Change Ahead

To order additional copies, please contact us.
BookSurge, LLC
www.booksurge.com
1-866-308-6235
orders@booksurge.com

Change Ahead

Working In A Post 9/11 World

Dr. Pat Gill Webber

2005

Change Ahead

TABLE OF CONTENTS

SPECIAL RECOGNITION

This book would never have happened without two very special people. Although dozens of colleagues and friends helped make the book happen, two were there throughout and deserve special thanks and recognition. Simply put, they made the book possible and they made the book what it is. They are both in a sense my coauthors in this endeavor.

The first is Dr. Thanos Patelis. Thanos is a brilliant statistician, a wonderful thinker and educator whose work at the College Board and at many universities is respected and admired. His clear mind, and his ability to synthesize and organize cannot be overestimated. His help in shaping the ideas of the book, and most importantly his help in discovering the best ways to find the data we were looking for, made this book possible.

Dr. Thanos Patelis was my support, colleague, and partner in this endeavor. Without his hard work, advice, support, and strength this book would never have seen the light of day. Thank you Thanos.

The second person whose work made this book possible is Noël Appel. Noël is a woman of many talents—a writer, editor, and executive in development in her own right. Noël has been a help, support, and guiding light from the earliest days when I was starting to think about the book, pull together resources, and think through what I wanted to write about. Noël did many things in this book—she edited, worked to develop bibliographies, and oversaw and organized the whole writing process.

Noël Appel was my coach, colleague, and supreme helper in making this book possible. This is also your book Noël. Thank you.

WAYS TO READ THIS BOOK

Many people love to read research. More do not. Much of this book is a review of research we conducted and an analysis of what that research means. If you are a person in Human Resources management, a leader interested in the details of how one or another site or group responded to questions, a researcher or professor who wants to know the details—read the book cover to cover—you will love the detail, the graphs, and all the weight of research behind our end of book recommendations. You might also add your own thinking to our research findings and come up with some new and different ideas of how to use the research data for your own needs. We welcome and encourage such interaction with our work.

If you are a "bottom line" sort of person—a leader looking for an idea of what in the world your colleagues and staff are thinking, an answer to the question of whether or not people are change adverse, an individual wondering what others are thinking at work and if you are alone, or an organizational change leader looking for some clear and straight forward strategy advice that is based on reality and facts rather than just someone's opinions, you might want to look at specific portions of this book and get the key points we learned from our research initiative and consider our specific strategies based on the research results. Here is how to do that.

Read the Forward to know who Pat Gill Webber is. I wrote the vast majority of the book and am the key author. This tells you where I am "coming from" so you can understand my biases while reading the book. Read the Narrative Objective to understand what the research and the book was designed to do. Then read the synopsis and implications for Parts I, II, and III of the book which cover all the research we did to understand the world at the current time, what people are thinking about change, and how people are handling change at work. At that point proceed directly to Part IV to read the synopsis, the implications, and the whole chapter for specific recommendations based on our months and years of research and hundreds of hours of thinking. Finally, look at the synopsis of Part V which tells you about the references and resources available here. This recommended set of material is less than 60 pages. If you have the time or interest, you can go back into the first three parts to read the details of both phases of our research and our overview of the "Big Picture" as we call it, the details of the organizations we worked with in depth and the analysis of the populations we worked with—over 300 people in phase one and over 600 people in phase two.

We hope this helps you navigate the book and gain from it what you need and want. We hope as well that if you have any unanswered questions or want to share your thoughts or thinking on some aspect of the book, you will contact me at patgillwebber@drpatgill.com

Pat Gill Webber
Summer 2005

For Dennis
We love you and miss you. Your support early on meant the world to me and still does.

And, For Bill
For all we have shared, for all we are, and all we will be, thank you.

FORWARD

I have always been interested in the ways people change and grow to meet life's challenges. From the time I began teaching (1970) and counseling (1973), that interest has focused on helping individuals develop resilience and competence in work and success as a person in an increasingly complex world. After I obtained a second masters degree in business (1979), my work focused almost exclusively on the world of work, where helping individuals develop competencies and attitudes for success also meant helping the organization itself to survive and thrive.

This dual perspective of helping both individuals and organizations has become my life's work. It has continued to evolve over the decades along with the world of work. In response to those ongoing changes those of us in the developmental fields (both organizational development and personal transformation and development) continue to focus on how best to develop organizations—as well as leaders and staff—who have the capability to create more effective and efficient organizations to cope with increased competition and evolving global markets.

The impetus to write this book came about after the early dust had settled after the tragedy of 9/11. There was a sense that this unique event would be responsible for a deeper shift in individuals' thinking and responding to change. Inevitably, it seemed to me, these shifts in thinking would begin to influence the way people behave and cope with both disaster and other less tragic but not necessarily less individually traumatic events at their places of work.

After more than 30 years of working in organizations, it has become clear to some of us in the change management business that people were already evolving their thinking and attitudes toward work and their lives more broadly. Could 9/11 and its accompanying cultural changes tip the scales and hasten even broader changes in people's thinking and behavior that would influence their emotional intelligence, behavior, and adaptation to change at work? Are people's evolutions in perceptions and thinking being considered by organizations as they embrace needed change?

For a long time, many in the human resource development field have felt that the methods and approaches organizations employ to create and foster change, as well as the ways management deals with people and their livelihoods, were increasingly outdated. If for no other reason than that change initiatives often failed, we and others continue to believe that there needs to be continued attention not just to the need for change, but the way we organize or develop change. In *Terms of Engagement: Changing the Way We Change Organizations*, Richard Axelrod's critical work on changing the change paradigm introduced to a broader audience a new approach to change that at its core creates a wider circle of engagement and a more expansive method of change management. This work was an important part of the change literature, bringing to public awareness that the need for people to be adaptive and flexible extended to their organizations.

The need then for individuals to be more open to change and more mature in their thinking is a given if unstated assumption of personal and organizational change. My colleague, Dr. Thanos Patelis, and I believe that this was a missing piece in the current literature of personal and organizational change. Simply put, the need for people to be open to change appears to be a given, but we did not believe we had much data on how, if at all, individuals were evolving and shifting their perceptions about personal or organizational change. Without this data, people and organizations were left to make assumptions about attitudes and beliefs that might be outdated or incorrect. Although managers and leaders might think they know that folks don't like change, their knowledge of individuals' actual feelings and actions related to change were not, and are not, easily accessible.

Since the mid-90s, considerable work has focused on leaders and how they need to evolve to meet the needs of change and globalization. I have been involved in some of this movement. We know that competency models developed in the 70s and 80s were essentially incomplete as we faced the 90s and the early years of the 21st century. This updating of leadership models is a positive development in our field and is creating new and emerging approaches that reach beyond the good efforts of the previous decades. Managers and leaders remain the main means of culture-forming in organizations as well as the producers of bottom-line success or failure of any organization. Their influence on how organizations operate and facilitate change cannot be overestimated.

There has also been considerable focus on strategies of change and transformation which help shed light on approaches that work more effectively than others to create enduring organizations of value. Books like *Good to Great: Why Some Companies Make the Leap. . .and Others Don't* (Collins, 2001) and *What Really Works: The 4+2 Formula for Sustained Business Success* (Joyce, Nohria, 2003) discuss research that has provided approaches and strategies that enable organizations to meet the challenges of increased globalization. Complexity theory and science also entered the mainstream of business thought as sophisticated thinkers in organizations began to fathom the importance of massive shifts and nonlinear change that affect how change occurs.

But, as noted above, less attention has been paid to the shifting thinking patterns, developmental levels, and abilities to manage and deal with change of all staff. Dr. Patelis and I believe that this would be both an interesting and highly relevant area of inquiry. If, in fact, people at work were more or less open in their thinking regarding change, this information would support leaders who are attempting to create greater change and transformation. Such an inquiry would also help practitioners in the field who work with strategy approaches requiring involvement of all staff to make progress. Finally, it helps organizations' human resource strategies and approaches in areas as diverse as selection, recruitment, development, and reward, which need to consider the evolving nature of worker perceptions.

The point of writing the book was to reflect upon where people "are" in their thinking and openness to dealing with change, as well as assess their emotional intelligence as a means to implement appropriate behaviors for organizational and personal change and success. Secondly, this book would suggest ways that might be more helpful in working within organizations to create the processes and approaches to work, livelihood, and success that bring an organization to life and sustains its energy in ongoing and relentlessly changing times. The recommendations made would evolve from the data we gathered indicating what workers are able and willing to do based on where they "are." For while best practices may suggest one or another strategy, we wanted to know for sure what people were capable of given our research before we recommended any specific actions.

Change Ahead is a melding of two phases of research designed to explore the evolving thinking and emotional maturity and intelligence of people who work in organizations. The first piece is broad and includes a survey that sought a large diverse population of people in different age groups and parts of the country and the world who could share with us their thinking about change and behavior post-9/II. A series of interviews were also conducted to attain more in-depth insight into how people's lives changed after this tragedy.

The second part of the research was conducted at organizations where we tried to assess where people were in their work lives by understanding the specific conditions that existed in these organizations, and to consider people's emotional intelligence and reactions to change given those conditions.

We grounded both pieces in an overview of the current "Big Picture" of where the world is and where the world of work is. We felt this grounding and knowledge would provide a broad context upon which to see and understand the research data. In a sense, it is the broader framework which has set the stage and allowed for the current thinking and attitudes of employees today.

These two sets of data were then blended with our knowledge of the Big Picture to determine ideas about how change approaches and processes might need to evolve as people's own selves had evolved and what that might mean for organizations.

Finally, my coauthor and I collaborated to develop and share lessons learned that we thought would be broadly helpful moving forward.

It is our profound hope that this discussion of the changing workforce will bring about more research, thought, and reflection among practitioners of organizational and personal change. It is also our hope that it will add to our field's understanding of shifting perceptions and how important it is to consider these when working in organizations. Finally, we hope *ChangeAhead* enlightens the reader in their awareness of how they or others they know and work with may have changed personally post-9/11 (and sadly now post 7/7/05), and whether that change is consistent with some of our considered observations and analysis.

Pat Gill Webber
Summer 2005

NARRATIVE OBJECTIVE

The purpose of this book is to explore with the reader perceptions of life post-9/II, the current workforce and their evolving views on personal and organizational change, and their levels of emotional intelligence and capacity for coping with change and transformation in their work lives. It is the secondary purpose of this book to share our insights into the implications of this "shifting perspective" to help support more effective personal and organizational change needed in today's increasingly complex world.

It is our goal to reflect on the general results of a two-phase research process that was conducted as part of the preparation of this book. The first phase of research involved selected in-depth interviews and a survey of attitudes toward personal and organizational change post-9/II. It was not assumed that 9/II was a seminal event. We explored what changes, if any, the subjects felt were happening to them or to their feelings and behavior post-9/II. This process provided fascinating insights into the thinking of a broad range of people and an awareness of their openness to the research. Phase one also explored whether people had perceived in themselves some type of change that would predispose them to be more or less open to personal or organizational change.

Once the first phase of the research was complete in 2003, we worked with the data and began to sense its relevance to the world of individual work performance and organizational performance. We identified a real shift in people's understanding of themselves and what was important to them. And we felt certain that whether organizations of any type were paying attention or not, people's shifting ideas, beliefs, and behaviors were having a profound effect on the culture of organizations and their capacity to cope with planned or spontaneous changes. While it cannot be said that everyone was changed post the traumatic events of 9/II and the subsequent "war on terrorism," many were changed in subtle and not so subtle ways. These shifts in one's sense of self, of what one believes is important, were, in our view, an extremely relevant piece of information for organizational change professionals, as well as for all managers and leaders in organizations. If organizations are continuing to face radical changes in their respective markets—and there is no argument that they are—what happens to strategies and individual performance when people shift their thinking and feelings about what is important and worth a commitment?

The business literature has been quite helpful in providing a variety of excellent books and articles about strategies for change and new leadership approaches to take on the responsibility for these changes. There has been increasing emphasis as well on executive coaching strategies and the need for more coaching in light of shifts in people's perceptions and their need for change. However, we did not see books and articles which explored the relationship between what is new in the minds, hearts, and behaviors of workers at all levels and the impact of this on the creation of transformation and change in organizations. This represents a major missing link in the literature on organizational change and individual performance.

In Part I of the book we attempt to set the stage for the research results by considering the broader framework that our participants found themselves in during the first part of the 21st century. This helps explain some of why they may have responded to the research questions as they did. The results of the first phase of survey research are described in Part II. In Part III, we look at the workplace itself and explore workers' real reactions to actual organizational change. We also looked at their levels of emotional intelligence which indicate the behaviors they are capable of using and use to work, given the changes they are experiencing. While the first phase of the research asked and focused on what people feel, the second part focused on what their actual attitudes and skills are to cope with real change in actual work situations. This moved the research from opinion to skills. For while many may SAY they are pro-change the proof as it were is in the real world of work.

We end the book with suggestions for individuals at work, as well as organizational change agents, managers, and leaders who have the bulk of the responsibility to manage change. Leaders or consultants have the challenging task of providing expert counsel to and working jointly with individuals throughout the organization, transforming modern institutions of all types with the goal of helping them prosper in the 21st century.

It is our hope that by more closely understanding the mind shifts and current emotional and behavioral strengths of workers, efforts to create and sustain necessary change will be both easier to develop and more in keeping with the workers' needs and abilities. Greater alignment between workers and organizational strategies will result in improved organizations with less stressed, more productive workers. There is no argument that the world of business and nonprofits is enormously stressful and faster paced than ever before. Our goal is to help ease this pressure and support individuals who will be more productive if they work in less pressured and insecure workplaces. We also want to help organizational leaders who desperately need employees who are open and willing to participate in the changes that will ensure success in increasingly challenging markets.

We hope this book proves valuable to those in both the for-profit and nonprofit fields—in private industry and the public sector. No organizations are immune to change, and no individual who is employed can expect to work without fairly consistent changes of one type or another. Essentially we took a snapshot of people in the 2002 to 2004 timeframe and have attempted to share what are the critical trends in this population of workers. We hope that as a result of this discussion, a specific and textured conversation within your own organization will ensue. We further hope that this dialogue will enhance your knowledge of the challenges you face so that they can be addressed with a conscious understanding of where you and/or your employees are emotionally and behaviorally. This expertise related to the feeling and behaviors of you and your staff should play a critical role in influencing how your organization can thrive in the 21st century.

PART I

The Big Picture

SYNOPSIS AND IMPLICATIONS

People do not work or live in a vacuum. They live in a context—in a culture, a time, impacted by its issues and molded by attitudes prevalent in the society as a whole. They are also impacted by the context of the workplace and its leadership philosophy, strategies, and market approaches as well as an organization's unique culture. When we began our research into what people were thinking about change, and how they were dealing with change in their lives post 9/11, we felt it was imperative to have an understanding of the world they were living in and how it might be impacting their thinking and behaviors. To do that we essentially read about and then analyzed life in the United States in the early part of the 21st century, most especially as it relates to the workplace. It is not that we ignored the world at large—far from it. But we limited our close inspection to what was happening here, in the United States, and how this context would effect workers of all types in any organization including nonprofits and global enterprises. We focused on the big issues including globalization, terrorism, and the new unstable world it has created, the culture wars with their relatively new strong "right" leaning impact as well as the more open culture including the shift toward self-development, self-determination, and self-help. We explored the rise of spirituality and its implications. All of these forces were seen as impacting people and their mindsets. Mostly we felt that these forces were creating more sophisticated thinking, more open thinking patterns, and more maturity and complexity of thought—but we did not yet have the research to prove it.

In these four chapters of part one, we also considered the current workplace. We focused on strategies and markets that we saw as evolving and moving quickly and decisively to deal with pressures of globalization. We observed significant progress on creating organizations of all types with strong process orientations and a realistic view of competition. We saw too a lag in leadership and management styles and approaches.

We noted that despite vast improvements in many aspects of running organizations, the management and leadership often were not as educated and sophisticated in their thinking and approaches due to a lack of strong investment in making that happen. In an odd twist of events and implications, we saw organizations grappling with business realities in the broadest sense of that term, but we did not see an equal commitment to modern and more effective leadership and management in many organizations. We also touched on the explosion of technology and felt that its effect was far greater than many organizations may have thought—people exposed to technology at work use it more often and in broader ways than others. This explosion in the uses of technology we surmised was going to increase the mind sets and thinking of workers across the spectrum, making them more aware and more in touch with global realities, and more open minded and pro-change than their leaders or organizations might suspect.

The results of our overview of the world at large, or what we call "the Big Picture," set the stage for our first phase of research with people who we predicted would show more positive pro-change attitudes. We had no idea HOW pro-change those mind sets would be.

CHAPTER I

Background

To understand how working people may have evolved and changed in their perspectives, we felt it was necessary to discuss two areas that constitute the broader context of the workplace. We call this two-part context the Big Picture. First, we discuss the economic, political, and cultural context. Second, we discuss organizations as they are currently constituted and how they have evolved in the last few decades. Specifically in this second section of Part I, we will focus on three core issues related to organizations. These three areas are: the state of strategy and markets; the role of leadership and the nature of employee and management relations; and the area of change and technology. This context explains in part why workers may feel or think as they do. Later, in Part III we discuss the specific situations of the work sites where we conducted our research. Organizational contexts, the Big Picture, and the specific work situation of any given company are extremely relevant to consider as organizations and individuals move forward.

People do not operate in a vacuum. Context is highly relevant although not entirely sufficient to understanding people's perceptions. We know from current thinking on organizations that randomness and complexity are more of a reality than order and consistency. As theorists and practitioners of "the new science" tell us, organizations are unique and made up of multiple variables that make them different. Simple rules of cause and effect, efforts at standardization, or even best practices are not always relevant to a deep understanding and leadership of today's organizations. The fact that all organizations are unique and continually reshaping themselves is a critical, somewhat obvious but sometimes overlooked consideration in implementing change strategies. Although lessons learned and best practices can be helpful, they can never be sufficient in developing change strategies for a specific organization. We hope our research and shared insights will remind individuals and professionals seeking to take part in personal change or those that are trying to influence change within organizations that to ignore either the broader context that people work and live in, or a specific organizational context that is ever-shifting, could doom an otherwise carefully thought out and well designed change strategy.

Our Big Picture, as noted, is a combination of the world at large and the organization at large. In both cases we observed a number of large scale shifts well documented in many finely researched books addressing these aspects of modern life. We reference a number of these works in our bibliography. Since we are not experts in these areas, we claim no unique insights into how the world at large has changed or how cultural trends have evolved, but rather seek to share our informed understanding based on others' work in these areas.

We looked to Thomas Friedman and other societal observers and experts to inform us of the move from the cold war to the world of terrorism, and from a world shaped by division to one shaped by integration. We reviewed political books like *The Emerging Democratic Majority* (Judis, Nohria, 2003) and *What's the Matter with Kansas?: How Conservatives Won the Heart of America* (Frank, 2004), as well as the enormous outpouring of analysis after the 2004 Presidential election that demonstrated shifts from the liberal to conservative (and in some cases back again) to gain insight into the evolving mindset of voters and citizens about what constitutes effective and appropriate action for our government. To understand the forces that were changing cultural norms and social trends outside of business, we looked at the vast self-help and personal transformation literature, from Melody Beatty to Louise Hay, from Dr. Deepak Chopra to Dr. Wayne Dyer, and from the hot-selling Christian books like the "left behind" series to reflections on changing structures of more mainstream religions.

In terms of business literature, we considered strategy books like *What Really Works: The 4+2 Formula for Sustained Business Success* (Joyce, Nohria, 2003) and *Good to Great: Why Some Companies Make the Leap. . .and Others Don't* (Collins, 2001), leadership books such as *Primal Leadership: Realizing the Power of Emotional Intelligence* (Golemna, McKee, Boyatzis, 2002), and countless articles such as the special January 2004 issue of the Harvard Business School related to the topic. We also considered *The 8th Habit: From Effectiveness to Greatness* (2004), Stephen Covey's new book, which does a terrific job of summarizing large-scale changes in organizational life and the challenges resulting from those shifts. We considered the new science's effect on business thinking, as well as strategy and trends in business from executive coaching to an over-reliance on technology. As with the first section of our work focusing on the broader context, our purpose was to consider consistent trends and conditions likely to have shaped the Big Picture and hence impacted our subjects' feelings, thinking, and perceptions of change and reactions to change.

Our plan was not to offer a review of all the history of the recent past, nor to write an extensive research review of these topics as they might exist in a doctoral dissertation, but rather to illuminate the broad context that workers found themselves in during the early 21st century. Our intention was also to create a springboard for study by a particular organization that might be more or less impacted by a given situation. It will be important to organizations engaging in any change or transformation effort to also spend time studying changes in their industry. This is a major issue that would and does create unique conditions that impact all workers and leaders. By sharing the perspective we developed about the Big Picture, we also hope to clarify some of the conclusions we draw later in the text.

We began our research post 9/11 when we sensed as did many others that life and work as we have known it in the United States had changed profoundly. First we considered how 9/11 and other events of recent history have changed people's thinking and priorities. We thought that perhaps these changes would begin to show up in new trends and ways of perceiving work that might help both individuals and organizations learn to be more productive and effective despite increasing discordant and stressful times.

People have been impacted and influenced in their thinking and perceptions by many aspects of modern life. From a change in cohort thinking (boomers versus Xers and Echo Boomers) to the catastrophe of 9/11, to their own personal evolution and journeys in life, people are evolving in what we see as appropriate ways. We also reviewed *Changing Minds: The Art and Science of Changing Our Own and Other People's Minds* (2004), Howard Gardner's brilliant work on the cognitive nature of changing one's own and other's minds. This seminal work also informed our thinking on how best to use people's current thinking and perceptions to achieve influence in change situations.

Our research supports our belief that many workers have evolved away from the stereotype of the change adverse and change resistant worker who is fear based and needing management to spin the reality of what is going on in organizational life. While some people (maybe a new minority?) may still strongly resist innovation, change, and complexity, many workers in organizations are more independent, interdependent, and sophisticated thinkers with some greater degrees of emotional intelligence and openness to change than commonly thought by the majority. Our work suggests that some of that evolution is due to the influences of the Big Picture as we have described it.

Conversely, we observe that the Big Picture demonstrates how some trends stem from what we consider an improper use by media or organizational leaders to mislead and damage people's ability to think and grow personally and professionally. The "success" of scare tactics or other strategies to gain political or personal advantage has always been available to those who wish to manipulate. But with current technologies such as the web, and the concentration of media ownership, it is now possible to attempt and sometimes succeed in creating trends that run counter to the best long-term interest of individuals and organizations.

In summary, many people at work are being underestimated. This may create a problem for the new minority—those who, despite Big Picture and interpersonal changes, have themselves remained untouched by broader trends. This new minority of those not open to change may be the biggest issue with which we all need to face. We will address this issue in the last chapter of the book where we consider implications of our research. Our book will illuminate what we have learned about today's workers, and how both organizational leaders and individual workers will benefit personally and professionally from using that awareness to better thrive rather than just survive in these tumultuous and exciting times.

CHAPTER 2

The Economic, Political, and Cultural Context

Globalization

There are no economic trends more influential on organizational life than the rise of globalization. "Globalization is the comprehensive term for the emergence of a global society in which economic, political, environmental, and cultural events in one part of the world quickly come to have significance for people in other parts of the world...the most dramatic evidence of globalization is the increase in trade and the movement of capital....by the early part of the 21st century more than 1.5 trillion worth of yen, euros, dollars and other currencies were traded daily to support expanded levels of trade and investment." (William K. Tabb for Microsoft Encarta Online Encyclopedia 2004.)

Organizations have come to regard the global nature of business as a given. Competition, workforce deployment, markets, and strategies are all affected by global trends. Even organizations that might not seem to be directly effected are impacted. Universities, hospitals, schools, nonprofits, government agencies, or even local small businesses from retail to home improvement feel the pinch of globalization in comparison with other nations, similar global enterprises, businesses, and the flow of employees into different fields. No organization is immune. Only the most naïve would ignore global trends within one's industry or career area. The good news is, finding this information about globalization or trends (or any subject for that matter) has never been easier. Increasingly, data suggests many workers are availing themselves of this type of information.

The growth of the web (which allows instant access to information exceeding any library) and its impact on communications, commerce, and popular culture cannot be overestimated. No industry is untouched, no work or career unchanged by the constant growth of the web and its transformational power to share information. Where one used to need know-how and time to investigate an issue, pursue leads into a story of interest to one's field, or do a research paper on the expanded industry one is in, all are now easily done with the support of nearly universal search tools like Google or Microsoft. Of course we are aware

9

that a digital divide still exists. However, in terms of our research, we focused on working people who today have access to computers and the Internet. All of our own research was conducted on the Internet through secure links to surveys. The only exceptions were in-depth interviews which were conducted in person or by phone.

One must assume that people who are exposed to computers at work are using the web. In fact research indicates that the greater exposure to technology at work or school, the greater the general use and confidence in using technology. Organizations would be wise to stay in touch with the depth and breath of what people are looking at and learning from. It is not at all uncommon for staff to be more informed on what is happening in their organizations via a web search than their own management. If something about one's organization is out on the web, wise management assumes some if not many employees know it. Keeping "secrets" has never been more difficult or futile. We see increased interest in and use of the web as a means of staying on top of trends and workplace issues. With diminishing confidence in leaders and managers, workers are getting information they need through the web.

The danger is the unregulated "standing in front of the water cooler" nature of information accuracy on the web. While theoretically "news" or information presented on a news channel or in a book or credible newspaper may have some source of validity, there is no editorial consistency on the web. Any and all informed or ill-informed opinions are out there for consumption. However, despite significant inaccuracies and outright lies, many people's sophistication is apparent in their own screening of information. While it is likely true that some if not many are ill served by web information that is hugely biased or unsubstantiated, this is not significantly different than people seeking only to see or hear other forms of information that coincides with their own already formed opinions.

Research has suggested that those watching Fox or CNN are more conservative or more liberal respectively. It seems people tend to be drawn not to objective reality—if any such thing existed—but rather to the particular point of view one already has developed. We recommend a thorough reading of both the concept of paradigms as presented by Thomas Kuhn's text *The Structure of Scientific Revolutions (1996)*, and the popularization of the concept developed expertly by Joel Barker's book *Paradigms: The Business of Discovering the Future (1993)*. Collectively they provide an excellent understanding of the dilemma people face when trying to confront or undo the established paradigms of any person or group. We again mention *Changing Minds: The Art and Science of Changing Our Own and Other People's Minds (2004)*, Howard Gardner's book, since that is also relevant in terms of understanding the formation of ideas and opinions as well as difficulties in changing such once formed.

It appears then that there is a dichotomy. On the one hand, we are finding many people whose sophistication and critical thinking is evolving, while at the same time there is an ever-present danger that people's established ways of thinking and seeing the world might make them unable to see critically around some important issues in their personal or professional lives. This attempt to change or shift people's paradigms is often the task of change management programs or other efforts to reinvent institutions. It is no wonder the challenge is so great and the uncertainty of reaching people so complex. However, if we are finding that change is more appreciated and understood by people, and there is the use of more change strategies that actually involve individuals rather than just inform or try to persuade them, then the dilemma or dichotomy is not as much of an issue or challenge.

For the majority of American workers, there is a recently developed perception that jobs, work, careers, and the nature of organizational life has been and will be forever altered due to the forces of globalization. No longer just a threat to blue collar jobs, many in white collar professions worry about the future and the availability of good paying and secure positions. In many ways, the very idea of a high paying secure job is itself an anachronism. People appear to understand at some visceral level that security comes from their own planning and responsibility for their work and career and not from any organization or job. People expect to have multiple positions, a career that has stops and turns, and likely will involve more than four or five organizations.

When Enron collapsed, many were shocked—especially those who had convinced themselves that this new organization was secure despite it not following the older established rules of what made sense in business. Many others who were skeptical from the start of "new economy paradigms" were simply not surprised. This understanding of both the potential for greed or malfeasance (Enron, WorldCom) and more benign but nonetheless enormously powerful economic forces larger than any organization or company (like outsourcing, downsizing, and productivity improvements resulting in fewer unskilled workers) seems to have risen as the forces of globalization have continued to influence the nature of work, the availability of work, and the remuneration for work. Peter Drucker, the 95-year old management guru, tells *Fortune* magazine in October 2003 that, "The dominance of the United States is already over. What is emerging is a world economy of blocs represented by NAFTA, the European Union, and ASEAN. There's no one center in this world economy. India is becoming a powerhouse very fast. The medical school in New Delhi is now perhaps the best in the world. And the technical graduates of the Institute of Technology in Bangalore are as good as any in the world." (Downloaded from www.freerepublic.com.)

Many are listening, responding, and understanding that forces of globalization—both good and bad, are influencing all aspects of life and work.

Closely related to the issue of globalization is the issue of diversity. We no longer live in a black and white world. We live in a global world. It is not unusual to work with people of varied religions, varied backgrounds, and enormously diverse cultures. Where once we would conduct management training workshops and seminars with primarily male audiences dotted by a few scattered women and people of color, the entire map of executives and workers has grown like a giant mosaic of the world at large. In a recent workshop of 50 new young leaders at a global pharmaceutical firm, Africans, Asians, Australians, Europeans, and Americans of every hue and background were the norm. Diversity is no longer "how the races need to get along" but rather a new way of thinking about and learning to interact with people who are diverse in multiple ways, the least of which is skin color. Stereotypes and simple assumptions about people's backgrounds can no longer be accepted. The range of differences and the range of cultures is just too great.

In response to this increased diversity, several things are happening. First, the public at large is becoming more open and accepting of difference. Even with all the hoopla over gay marriage, increasingly large numbers of people are supportive of this; the last of the "discriminated against groups" is gaining solid support from increasing numbers of people. We have noticed a wide spread phenomenon in the Echo Boomer generation—where issues of race and culture were often areas of stress for the boomers, this younger generation has grown up with diversity and often easily adapts and accepts differences as a given. They find it easy to work for people of different genders and cultures since they were raised with more diversity in their schools, neighborhoods, and via the media and their culture which is ever more diverse. Younger people need help with their emotional intelligence, but many seem to think the older generation's issues of problems with different races is a thing of the past and not in keeping with their ideas of what is appropriate, sensible, or useful. It has become a more diverse world, and for the most part, especially younger people seem more than OK with that change.

We find that the more people use the Internet, the more accepting of diversity they become. What we used to call "pen pals" are now every day email friends in different countries, and meeting and interacting with various types of people is everyday news on the net. Where once one may never have met or worked with people in another place, today we are commonly interacting across the globe electronically, and finding it challenging but not impossible to do so.

The challenge, of course, is learning not just to be color or culture blind—a somewhat ubiquitous ideal of an earlier age, but rather to be more adept at working with a widely diverse workforce and personal groups in any setting. However, beyond getting along, we want to create an awareness of the unique value of diversity. Likely there are few historians that would not acknowledge that one of the best things about the United States has been its acceptance of diversity and its use of the best of all cultures. We know that we can achieve greater and richer innovations and results of all types when we collaborate with others who have a different way of seeing and being in the world. From music to business strategies, the most creative work is usually one that has a wide input from diverse thinking and diverse input.

Part of our own work has been to discuss issues of diversity in a group setting—not by the old means of telling what different people think and how to behave, but rather through having people share their own stories. It is through these means that people learn that diversity involves everyone—that white men are just as diverse as others in the way they process information and think about issues. Diversity is a complex concept that has clearly grown beyond the original concept that diversity means different races or national origins to a more sophisticated view that diversity means differences of every type—especially differences in thinking and understanding issues.

Diversity is both a challenge and a built-in plus to the new age of globalization. Without a deeper understanding and acceptance of others, we cannot and will not prosper. But too, there are dangers in not knowing when lines need to be kept in place. Businesses need global collaboration, but they also need to design products and services that meet unique conditions and cultures. The creation of one world culture is not yet a universal aim, although a common and shared approach to world problems is a remaining aspiration for most people in the world.

The War on Terrorism

The history of the mid-twentieth century to the present can be told from the viewpoint of governments and their interactions. After WW2, the cold war was the major framework of geo-politics. The nation state was the unit of action and the world was roughly divided into two armed camps headed respectively by the United States and the Soviet Union.

Politics both right and left had to deal with this political reality. The primary metaphor as described by Thomas Friedman in *Longitudes and Attitudes: The World in the Age of Terrorism* (2003) was "division." We were divided from the Soviet Union and its allies in our views of freedom, our values on personal liberty, and our physical presence. If they were there, we weren't, and vice versa. The Berlin Wall was the visual symbol of the Cold War. Some of us living and working in these times may remember the Bay of Pigs and the days when war with the Soviet Union seemed inevitable. We remember childhoods filled with nuclear bomb drills that sent us to scoot under our desks. Years later we realized the foolishness of this effort, but then it supported our thinking that the world was a dangerous place and that clearly we were the good guys and the Soviet Union was the bad. Like the cowboys and Indians depicted in westerns of our youth, good and bad were often complete opposites with little consideration of any middle ground or concepts like multiculturalism. The most common perception of the time was that violence or war was always possible, and that if it did occur it would be fought in some type of conventional way between warring countries, or in one or another place outside of the United States and contained.

In the world order of today, the United States remains the only real super power. Depending on one's politics and understanding of recent history, one can either believe we have handled this mantle well, or dishonored it. But in either case, the supremacy of the United States has come with a twist: although we may be the only remaining super power, we are not safe from terrorism and we do not control violence and "going to war" as we once did—or any country did.

The role of the state per se has diminished due to the power of the web and instantaneous communications. One man, or many small groups of men and women, can and do have the power to change lives, to alter situations, to take power into their own hands, or to produce terror. Where once "the enemy" meant a country or set of countries, we now can have groups or subgroups who decide to "fight us" due to any number of real or perceived issues, policies they deem unfair, or simply arrogant or grossly misguided thinking which appears probable in the case of the 9/11 disaster.

9/11 impacted people. Our research and much other research indicated that people's sense of security and peace of mind was forever altered. To those who were not changed, it is often because they somehow knew either through direct understanding and study that the world had been changing over a long period of time, and that it was not surprising that at some point terror would be in our own backyard. In one of our in-depth interviews, we talked with a person who considered himself a world citizen. His perception was that 9/11 was inevitable due to our government's foreign policies and history. This was in sharp contrast to another individual who felt that the war on terror was really a war of religious belief that pitted the Islamic peoples of the world against the Christian ones. One has to wonder if the recent (7/7/05) bombings in London would further influence this gentleman's view, or the other. In any case, it is clear from ongoing events, that terrorism is an ever-present reality and will, in our view, continue to create feelings and opinions that are strongly felt and deeply disturbing for many people.

While either view would likely be considered "extreme" by many, there is no doubt that the reasons for terror are not simple to understand or control. While some would state with certainty that the reason for terror is perceived unfairness in United States policies in the Middle East, particularly the Palestinian issue and the ongoing war in Iraq, others are just as clear that what has created terror-ism or the new terrorism is a hatred of who we are and what we have achieved. That simply, some Islamic people are unwilling to accept their own errors of judgment and policy that have created ongoing poverty and lack of progress in their own countries. To these people who see flaws in Islam itself or some of its proponents, our values and beliefs in freedom, equality of women, and an open society are what creates a hatred and desire to kill us.

Regardless of why there is a potential for more terrorism on our own soil, or in places all over the globe, the reality is that now that 9/11 (and 7/7) has occurred, we can never again believe it isn't possible for violence to come within the United States borders or any place around the world. Since Bin Laden has yet to be captured and his stated goal is an even bigger 9/11, we can assume something could happen again to disturb our way of life. It is hoped that the creation of a new organization for intelligence will lessen this threat, but it is hard to believe even with substantial changes that there is no likelihood of violence. Whether for reasons like religious bigotry and fanaticism or of perceived injustice or just jealousy, the threat of terror is part of people's lives globally. Religion and land/resources have long been top reasons for wars, violence, or terror; the difference today is the ability of fanatic groups of any kind to reach out via the web and other communications to both create more terror and communicate about it to its own constituencies and those they threaten.

It is clear that terror played a role in the election of 2004. Regardless if one voted, or whom one voted for, the politics of the campaign included many references to this new state of affairs. It seems somewhat self evident that a fear of future terror attacks, or a worry that more terror could occur, caused some people to vote either for Kerry or Bush, believing that their policies would create "more or better safety." By connecting to people's fears, the politicians were on safe ground. This confirms our finding and that of others that there continues to be a sense of unease in the new world order. There is no doubt that the fears associated with 9/11 and the uncertainty that it has created has influenced many to desire more protections. In a recent job satisfaction report (Society for Human Resource Management (SHRM) and CNN*fn*'s *Job Satisfaction Series: Job Compensation/Pay Survey* (Report 2004) covering the top five aspects of job satisfaction for employees by gender, both men and women listed "feeling safe" as a top element of job satisfaction. For those in the human development field long familiar with Abraham Maslow's hierarchy of needs, this data is not surprising. In his well-known work, people have a hierarchy of needs that starts with safety and security. In many ways, the advent of terrorism demonstrated by 9/11 created for some a reversal from attention to higher needs for socialization and actualization—a broader humanistic agenda personally, to one that focuses first and primarily on safety.

Businesses have had to respond to these needs for safety by spending increased amounts of money on safety issues. They also continue to face increased technology costs associated with protecting systems and people as well as increased focus on protecting global assets. Staffing and talent management has also been effected as more people refuse to work in what they perceive to be unsafe environments. Increased anti-Americanism is another factor that adds to feelings of lack of safety for people who work with global businesses that are primarily seen as United States organizations. Terrorism as a factor in the Big Picture appears to be something that should continue to influence people for the foreseeable future.

We end this section with a caveat. For while safety, security, and what we in the United States have come to call "the war on terror" is a major factor in our political landscape, the world at large has not really bought into our overall thinking of this as a worldwide issue. America's central preoccupation with the war on terror is not widely shared, and in fact can be seen as isolating us from the world at large. This suggests that the United States' current policies may yet shift again as either the current administration becomes more connected to others around the globe, or others take political power and choose to create greater alignment with other sections of the world. If that is the case, the environment of our workforce may shift again, dropping the preoccupation with safety further down the list of issues.

"The cold war world adhered to a simple paradigm of free societies, led by the United States, confronting Communism, with its headquarters in the Kremlin. But for all of President Bush's attempts to frame the current conflict against Islamic terrorism as one of equality epochal and all-enveloping proportions, it is now clear that the world has resisted such a single, overarching framework. In wide swaths of the southern hemisphere, including Africa and Latin America, the central preoccupation is economic development and trade. In Asia the main focus is on China rising, with India not far behind. In Europe, the bulk of political energy is still absorbed by the vast experiment in transnational governance and the banishment of war that is the European Union." ("The World: The War on Terror; An Obsession the World Doesn't Share" by Roger Cohen for *The New York Times*, December 5, 2004.)

Cultural Trends

The last election seems to leaves little doubt that the United States continues to be culturally divided. It also appears that the political parties themselves are also more divided, with strong core bases of voters that have almost opposite views on many critical issues. Voting patterns indicate that there are fewer politicians who stray from their party's position on any given issue. Whether it is the war in Iraq or abortion rights, health care policy or safety and security, there is division in how best to address and develop answers to these pressing national concerns. The discussion of the "red states" versus the "blue states" has continued since the election, giving rise to a perception that culturally the nation is divided into two groups: one more secular, accepting of diversity of all types, and concerned with issues like social justice and environmental security; the other more likely to distrust any large government programs like the tax system or social security, is conservative on social issues like gay marriage, and supportive of a foreign policy that is less likely to consider international alliances than what our current leaders in the executive branch consider right or wrong, just or unjust.

This cultural divide has been the butt of jokes and serious analysis, but we are not completely convinced that the divisions are as set in stone as some might believe. For example, there is now some confusion about who owns which values and positions between the parties. While the party of fiscal restraint more recently used to be the Republicans, with the Democrats favoring greater spending, the exact opposite has been happening in the last few years. We do not understand this as a fundamental change on either side but rather a shifting case of funding of policies on one or the other side. While Democrats might favor increased funding for the environment, more funding for diverse energy alternatives, scientific research, and education, the Republicans favor increased spending on the war in Iraq and simultaneously lowering taxes, especially for upper income tax payers and corporations that they believe create jobs and therefore help the economy. We like to think there is enormous overlap and room for common ground. For instance, there are likely an equal number of Republicans, Democrats, Independents, or nonvoters who would like to see smaller deficits regardless of how the government accomplishes that task. We also see a coming together and much crossover in the social security debate, indicating that many Republicans and Democrats are finding their constituencies of all persuasions concerned about the President's ideas of the privatization of some part of the system.

While we cannot contradict data that appears to suggest a divided nation, it is our sense that there is a core of shared values and culture that covers both the red and blue states. Perhaps it is a combination of pragmatism, a belief in the rights of individuals to be successful in their own ways, and a sense that everyone ought to be able to get a shot at opportunity, education, and "the American dream." There is also a large amount of shared patriotism and respect for soldiers who serve our country on both sides of the divide. There is as well a sense that it is important to take action to create a nation that reflects values of decency, fair play, and respect for the individual and her/his rights. With the recent tsunami tragedy, we once again see the enormous generosity and coming together of all types of Americans. The desire to do good deeds and be good is strong in our culture and transcends all political differences. The working together of former Presidents Bush and Clinton represents to us the model of this distinct set of American traits and represents the best of what is possible when the common decency and compassion of the American people is utilized in a productive manner.

The divisiveness of the last election may be the result of any number of factors, from the rise of the right-leaning media to longer evolving trends which suggest that younger people and single women continue not to vote in numbers that match their portion of the population. This is relevant particularly as it relates to understanding the workplace. It is likely that workers have been impacted by these issues and have strong feelings that need to be considered carefully when one is working with groups of people in complex organizations. No assumptions should be made about how staff or employees may feel or think about certain key issues. Our research suggests there is an enormous need for leaders of all types who can bring people together. Politicians like United States Senator John McCain and United States Senator Barack Obama represent those types of leaders who seem to have broad appeal. In businesses and nonprofits alike, leaders who can get people to rise above differences to feel excitement and passion about the mission and vision of their organizations can help mitigate these cultural divisive feelings that have impacted workers at all levels.

The role of religion is also playing a part in the diversity of the nation. There are more Muslims than Episcopalians, the religion of the "founding fathers." While the developed world is generally less religious than the underdeveloped world, the gross exception is the United States with the largest number of practitioners of all types of religion. While some may feel that the Christian conservatives had an unprecedented rise in power in the last election, it is equally true that religions of all types are growing their bases of participants.

Along with the continued influence of religions of all types is the ever-increasing rise of spirituality and its impact on all aspects of people's lives. This rise in attention to issues of spirit has created new ways of thinking about meaning and effectiveness in people's lives. Magazines like *Spirituality and Health* and continuing growth of alternative ways of studying and understanding how to bring people together and fight common problems, indicate a constantly increasing number of people who are open to new ways of looking at their lives, their faith, and the application of these ideas to their work as well as personal lives. We see the acceptance and appeal of sites like beliefnet.com which covers all religions of the world as an example of how people of all traditions and backgrounds are looking to share what is best about the spirituality and approaches of their faiths to bringing about better conditions and better tolerance around the world.

"Spirituality at work" is a trend, and has been noted as such by the *New York Times*, the *Wall Street Journal*, *Fortune* and National Public Radio. It remains, of course, somewhat of a controversial and complex topic since the term spirituality is so broad and the applications so diverse. Employees want to bring their whole selves to work. This creates challenges for leaders who need to consider how to engage the whole person, show respect and tolerance for diverse religious views, and maintain a strong division between Church and State. Experts in the field, such as Harvard Business School senior lecturer Dr. Laura Nash and Os Hillman, the director of the International Coalition of Workplace Ministries, feel that the trend was created and driven by the baby boomer generation who rebelled against religious conformity and instead began to revere "respect for the sacred self." (Training and Development, November 2004, pgs. 17-19.)

While 9/11 increased people's interest in their families, it also gave rise to more thought about spirituality and "what's most important in life." Since spirituality often links to more community-based activities, this increase in spirituality would seem to be a good thing. It seems, however, that at the same time there is more religious diversity and increased interest in spirituality, there is also a decline in many community-based activities. Whether due to 24/7 work lives or other pressures of modern life, or just a changing focus on the self and one's own family, some types of connection and community seem to be decreasing in our lives. This trend may begin to reverse itself as more people move to exurban areas beyond the suburbs and develop more ties to smaller towns and communities.

It may also be that although traditional types of connections and volunteer activities are decreasing, connection to others through the web has increased and people are linking with those with whom they share common volunteer or socially conscious interests. Organizations like MoveOn.org and hundreds of new charities are using the web to engage people in both practical and spiritual ways. Through organizations focused on issues from spirituality to helping our troops overseas, research and science to shared parenting tips, empowerment for the disabled to global dating and mating sites, strong connections have developed online, creating new types of communities that, as noted, may well be taking the place of older "place based" organizations of the 50s and 60s.

The cultural landscape is also shaped by several other large trends. As the baby boom generation gets closer to retirement, we see Generation X and Y coming forward with more interest in work-life balance. This can be illustrated by the fact that for the first time since 1976, the labor force participation rate of mothers with infant children declined in 2002. The SHRM Research (2004) pointed out that this interest in establishing more of a work-life balance is shared by men as well as women. However, since the Generation X group is not that large, the impact on work and its need to have more family-friendly policies may not happen until the later Generation Y has children. The idea of work being the center of people's lives is definitely passé. Most of the younger generations are clear that work is necessary, important, and possibly critical to one's dreams and aspirations, but work is not a life—and a life without ties, connections, and family is not worth living.

Education presents some interesting insights into our evolving culture. While the workplaces of the current time and future require more and better skilled workers, our efforts to improve education in the United States are decidedly mixed. While women are obtaining increased degrees and credentials, men are not. Where once international students were anxious to come here for college or graduate school, less of these students are doing this, causing real concern in the college community. Also it appears that the number of people obtaining college degrees is remaining constant despite the need for more educated workers. This may well be due to constantly rising costs of education and people being unwilling to take on large loans even if they are the "cheapest and best loans out there."

Our public schools may be trying to "leave no child behind," but there remains a crisis in the quality of our schools and educational resources. A recent study by the Organisation for Economic Co-operation and Development suggests that the United States, while spending more than other nations, has lower graduation rates than other developed nations. In addition, it further made the point that our educational success rates of students were particularly poor in math and science. If these educational trends continue, the United States may continue to lose well paying jobs to nations like India who are continuing to graduate more and better educated students. In February of 2005, Bill Gates, the founder of Microsoft, gave a blistering indictment of education to the governors of the United States and committed funds from his foundation to begin to address what he sees as the failures of the country to provide decent educations to the vast majority of its citizens. He is not alone in perceiving the dangerous situation the country will face if it continues to fail in providing more broad, high quality education.

The educational crisis seems to be intersecting with business and workplace needs. There continues to exist a mismatch between skills needed for jobs and people available. "In the decade following 2010, the portion of the population under age 45—the principle talent pool for managers and workers—will begin shrinking by 6 percent annually. In other words, structural demographic forces are now in place for a real war for talent that could continue for 20 years following 2010. ... As the skilled people who run United States corporations retire and the number of younger entry-level workers continues to fall, the effects of the great mismatch of skills and jobs will intensify. Unemployment will drop as jobs go unfilled and some businesses may leave the United States entirely in search of highly skilled, job-ready workers elsewhere." (*Training*, January 2005, pg. 35.)

CHAPTER 3

The Nature of the Organization

Strategy and Markets

As noted, the single greatest ongoing phenomenon impacting organizational strategy and markets is globalization. In response to this challenge, there has been a change in the approaches of organizations toward developing strategies and engaging with markets. Strategies that emphasize focus and tightly constructed and implemented missions and visions have brought more people into the process of active engagement in businesses and organizations. This has been a good thing. However, if other statistics are to be believed, despite efforts of organizations to include and educate people about their industries and tie folks into the key decisions of the enterprise, small numbers of employees truly feel engaged at work. In the opening to his new book, *The 8th Habit: From Effectiveness to Greatness* (2004), Stephen Covey shares the analysis of the Harris Interactive who recently polled 23,000 U.S. residents working in key industries. The results were shocking—only 37% had a clear understanding of what their organization is trying to achieve, and only one in five were enthusiastic about the goals of their team or organization.

In reality, the last ten years has been a time of survival and profound shifts. Globalization has created brutal competition in most markets, including nonprofits. With these challenges have come increased government regulation, post scandals of the recent past, and the realities of living in a post 9/11 world. These somber realities have caused many businesses to focus on what they saw as essentials—keeping their stockholders happy if they had them, or keeping the marketplace pleased with their product and service offerings. Less attention was paid to culture, appropriate motivation, and engagement strategies with people, despite years of research demonstrating its importance, and notwithstanding the enormous lip service that leaders of all kinds give to people and their issues.

The environment was just too tough to allow most executives and managers the comfort of being "side tracked" to implement needed and appropriate human, compassionate, and workable people strategies. Exceptions with wonderful stories are out there. A new book entitled *Joy at Work: A Revolutionary Approach to Fun on the Job* (2005) by Dennis W. Bakke about AES (a 40,000 person global energy enterprise) describes one of those organizations that took the radical approach of involvement and creating joy at work—achieved amazing results. However, this approach was rare. While HR folks tried to get to the table in larger numbers, and consultants continued to generate enormous resources that demonstrated the need for engagement and involvement, it never took center stage. Rather, short-sighted survival strategies—such as layoffs, inappropriate and failed mergers, new leader-generated change programs, and power grabs—became increasingly popular. Strong efforts to create pro-people, pro-learning, pro-high performance, and high engagement cultures did exist, particularly at winning firms. However, looking across strategies used by large numbers of organizations, those chosen were relatively standard market strategies of constant cost reduction, modified products, line extensions of existing products, attempts to make inroads with the emerging "upper class" of affluent Americans, low price and discount strategies, and expanded uses of all types of technology to replace workers when possible. These types of strategic efforts took the majority of resources from other strategies that would have put creative involvement of people, innovation, and productivity front and center.

A few terrible leaders of organizations in the last 10 to 15 years reached new levels of greed and arrogance as the culture of individualism and self-concern that is part of the broader American culture became part of the business culture as well. While this is changing somewhat in the early 21st century as contracts for CEOs are examined and reconsidered, it is clear from recent history that the guiding principle for some high profile leaders was their own enrichment rather than what was good for the majority of customers or employees. Again, this is not to suggest that this is a new phenomenon—greed after all has been around since the earliest of times—nor are we suggesting all leaders are greedy or that all executives took advantage of boards that would overpay to get them.

We are suggesting that this recent bout of greed took hold due to a number of forces, leaving the majority of workers less well off and less secure, while a few at the top were overly compensated and were depended on to make the difference that businesses felt the economy demanded. The idea of getting just the right leadership (the perfect CEO, for instance) became a strategy itself. Rather than relying on broader leadership and an approach that would have engaged a larger group in meeting market conditions, the strategy that took hold was to find the right players and hope they would make the right call and redirect failing or floundering organizations. It is hoped that a more realistic view of senior leaders will emerge, creating strategies and approaches that are more sensible, more broadly developed by the entire workforce within an organization, based on sound research of change management, and more likely to lead to better climates within organizations. It is not important or necessary to blame boards or leaders. It is, however, helpful to suggest that better strategies will emerge when organizations provide more security and more engagement to broader numbers of people, and when they spread compensation in ways that encourage deeper commitment to organizational goals.

While these failures existed, some better strategies also took hold during the period of the last ten plus years. Quality and reengineering, which had been around for decades, found real success in companies that at long last were trying these strategies as a means of continuing to drive out costs and waste. These strategies were also used to fix processes that were outdated or inefficient. While getting less publicity than at the height of the quality movement in the 1980s and early 1990s, quality initiatives were often quietly initiated and met with some success. Those organizations that continued to be innovative in the operations area, such as Dell and Wal-Mart, continued to beat their competitors consistently demonstrating that process improvements of any type can be a means of competitive advantage. In fact, quality process improvements, used consistently and with excellence, have and do help organizations sustain advantage in the marketplace.

Also tried with some success have been high performance culture strategies that are morphing into more concrete approaches to making high performance more predictable. Studies by groups like Booz Allen Hamilton and the Accenture Institute for High Performance Business are working to decode and simplify the areas that organizations need to focus on to be successful. As with books like *What Really Works: The 4+2 Formula for Sustained Business Success* (Joyce, Nohria, 2003), there are certain star performing companies (Toyota, Johnson & Johnson, and eBay, for instance) that have managed to innovate with excellence due to strategies that combine successful use of motivation tools, application of technology in strategic ways, focus on those few areas that will lead to success in a given business, and balancing long and short term results. Companies that used tried and true strategies such as refocusing on customers and sticking to their core businesses also succeeded.

Leadership: The Employee/Management Relationship

In talking about globalization, we covered what is the major change in organizational life in the last ten years. Speed and pressure to perform have multiplied. No matter the industry, productivity and rising expectations is the nature of modern working life. Workers feel the emphasis on productivity and push to do more with less. The knowledge workers of today are being expected to not just perform and increase productivity, but they are being counted on to be creative as well. This pressure to do more with less has directly impacted the employee/leadership relationship and unfortunately remains a problem for most organizations.

While the landscape of organizational life has changed due to globalization and increased needs to compete, the nature of organizations remain for the most part in the industrial age in terms of how they are organized and how management operates. While organizations are evolving through changing economic, cultural, and technological trends, organizational life has been slower to adjust to the need for work cultures that allow workers to be creative, contribute on an ongoing basis, and be truly engaged as full people excited by their work.

While employers have expected more from employees, they have consistently supplied less. Secure pensions, built-in cost-of-living increases, and ongoing and open opportunities for advancement are all less common than ever. Employees have become increasingly aware that their individual success is tied to the achievements of their organizations. They have come to expect less of the "perks" or benefits of an earlier time. However, one frustration that many employees feel, understandably, is that while they know their fate is tied to their organization's present situation, they seem less able to influence outcomes. Often poor leadership decisions (Enron, WorldCom, and Marsh & McLennan Companies, Inc. for example), poor market conditions (post 9/11 airlines for example), or just smarter competition (Dell, Wal-Mart, and Southwest Airlines) makes their individual efforts to help the organization seem less impactful. This leads to further alienation and turmoil in the workforce as employees wonder what they can do to protect their own interests more effectively in light of the current challenging economic developments. Furthermore, some employees are keeping up with the changes in business, the Internet and its impact on corporate cultures and business realities, as well as the competition and new global conditions. Keeping up with such dramatic changes has created a situation where some workers are less able to grasp these new realities, or if they grasp them to deal with the resulting more "Darwinian" work culture.

There have been dramatic increases in the attention paid to leadership education in many for profit and nonprofit organizations in the last decade. Leadership styles and approaches have been increasingly described in thousands of new books describing how best to lead in these tumultuous times. Having evolved from the more straightforward "how to" management development efforts of the 1970s and 80s, increased attention was placed on helping managers understand and develop missions, as well as visions and goals that linked to these objectives. Today's leaders must handle the basics like setting and articulating goals, hiring and firing staff, making day-to-day decisions, and listening and responding to employee needs. They also must be able to set and maintain momentum toward a vision, think critically and strategically not just locally, be a team leader and a team player, create and maintain a high performance culture, choose and develop talent for the organization—all the while being more self-aware and self-regulating, and willing to use collaboration to lead change successfully and influence beyond their own turf. Just reading the list is exhausting. The demands are greater than ever and there are fewer resources. This leaves a leadership crisis in many organizations, compounded by the inevitable loss of their most talented leaders as boomers are starting to retire.

More attention was paid to creating high performance cultures as the legacy of quality and process reengineering continued to encourage the empowerment of workers, as well as the involvement of teams to address organizational bottle-necks and increase productivity and innovation. Executive coaching came into its own and many executives began to avail themselves of this service. But despite its popularity and press, the actual numbers of people utilizing personal coaches or being impacted by new leadership strategies is relatively minor.

The combination of cyclical tough times, and limited resources especially for education and training, created a situation where leadership and manage-ment development is not a fully implemented approach in the bulk of companies outside of the top tier Fortune 50 or 100 and nonprofit top tier organizations. While many organizations dabbled in leadership and management development, the number of organizations who have a consistent and thorough training and education system in place for their management and leadership ranks remains relatively small.

Added to this gap between the literature of leadership and management training and the reality of its practice, the growth of newer technology firms and high tech companies with young and inexperienced management increased the gap between organizations with solid and professionally developed leaders and those that had whoever could handle the pace and push of the work culture. While leaders need increasing skills and models to handle increased complexity and growth of organizations, most leaders and managers outside of an elite few have minimal opportunities for leadership development, executive coaching, and ongoing support in their professional growth. From our vantage point, the needs are ever greater and the educational opportunities in shorter supply.

Competition has also led to increasing instability of work life, which con-tinues to make many workers extremely concerned with their survival. The natu-ral tendency to feel secure and safe has led some people to be overly cautious, trying to remain below the radar to avoid problems and potential loss of their job. While this is the exact opposite of the skills and attitudes needed, it is a nat-ural consequence of workers feeling exceedingly vulnerable in a fast-paced and competitive work world. While organizations need to support rather than stifle creativity and innovation through empowerment and improved human resources policies, many managers and leaders themselves lack the knowledge and skill to fully engage workers, treating them like disposable parts. The bottom line is that there is an increased need for new and evolved workplaces, but both workers and leaders are generally ill-equipped to make the necessary changes.

Finally, there is the issue of change management approaches. While many organizations have begun to implement one or another change initiatives, few if any have utilized newly recommended strategies that suggest more and broader engagement. As noted earlier, suggestions of a new paradigm of change that includes widening circles of constituencies are used very selectively, if at all. Most organizations are trying to cope with and address the need to change—few are successfully utilizing the advice of change experts who suggest more and ever-widening use of participation in these efforts to create successful and sustained improvement.

We do not want to appear totally without hope or suggest that many organizations are not attempting—whether through online learning or traditional learning—to close the gaps of skills and attitudes of both workers and leaders. But our general sense of the workplace indicates the needs are ever greater and the abilities to meet those needs are increasingly limited.

There is an irony here. While people appear to be shifting their perceptions on change and essentially are more open and willing to engage than ever before, organizations appear to be under-utilizing their people and continuing to underestimate the ability of workers to engage in and take part in helping to shape their futures. There is a saying in learning circles that "when the student is ready, the teacher will appear." It is evident that the student is ready, but the teacher is not allowing the student to learn or grow. Covey's *The 8th Habit: From Effectiveness to Greatness* (2004), presents an approach that supports many of our beliefs of fuller engagement. We are hopeful this book will achieve the success of Covey's first book, introducing more organizations to updated and effective methods for dealing with what we have found in our shifting perspectives of today's workers.

Change and Technology

With statistics showing that IM (instant messaging) will become an integral part of most workplaces in a few years, we can be sure that technology is everywhere part of the new workplace. According to a recent study by Gartner, Inc., about 70 percent of organizations are using instant messaging now; by the end of 2005, IM will be the primary way people interact electronically, surpassing email.

There is no doubt that increased means of communication, powered by and through technology, has swept the business world. Beginning in the 1970s and relentlessly into the 80s and 90s, the technology functions of organizations continued to expand, bringing increased means of productivity, increased ability to get and understand data, and tremendous changes in how work is done, organized, and processed. From supply chains to selection, from customer web sites to new purchasing systems, technology has transformed the corporation and nearly every nonprofit as well. More and more people work with colleagues they have never met or seen. People are part of teams that work exclusively over the net, and often there are customer and organizational bonds that are forged without anyone saying a word.

This is a profound change in the work world which will likely continue to expand. While collaboration is one of the essential new skill sets for successful work, the ability to collaborate is not what it needs to be—especially in complex organizations. Training in collaboration is increasing in organizations that value innovation, as it is determined that the personal skills needed to be an effective collaborator, and the tools needed to work across boundaries and cultures, is missing from many modern workers. Books like *Business without Boundaries: An Action Framework for Collaborating Across Time, Distance, Organization, and Culture* (Mankin, Cohen, 2004) are trying to help individuals and companies increase their effectiveness in this arena. At the same time that many people are connected exclusively by technology, the ability to interact in a meaningful way with others to either create possibilities or to imagine new ways of reaching people with services and products demands that we still work closely together. We still need to listen and engage with others in order to create successful businesses, projects, and lives. We have to find ways to do this with technology—and that remains a challenge.

While the use of technology has continued to reshape work, it has left some gaping holes as well. While communication tools and means of connection have never been greater, there is a sense that in many organizations there has been a loss of communication and connection. Ironically, more has not necessarily meant better. This, of course, is a frightening thought—we expect technology to be the answer to problems, not a creator of new ones, as it clearly is. And while there is little doubt that technology, properly used and applied, has made critical and amazing improvements to the bottom lines of many organizations, there clearly has been a fall-out with new challenges generated from too much email which distracts rather than supports work, to too much time on the Internet which decreases rather than increases people's productivity. Further, generations growing up with technology may find dealing with people "too slow" or "too boring" and have less adequately developed interpersonal skills that are desperately needed in today's organizations. Daniel Goleman's *Working with Emotional Intelligence* (1998) suggested a new way to measure and encourage intelligence in leaders and workers at all levels. He noted that the need for emotional intelligence is greater than ever, not lessened by technology. "The globalization of the workforce puts a particular premium on emotional intelligence in wealthier countries. Higher wages in these countries, if they are to be maintained, will depend on a new kind of productivity. And structural fixes of technological advances alone are not enough:...streamlining or other innovations often create new problems that cry out for even greater emotional intelligence." (p. 9.)

Technology continues to improve the means of communicating. From IM to ipods, the digital world is here and it is not likely to decline. The question is how this technology is impacting workers, their emotional intelligence, their ability to work well with others, and their ability to work coherently to achieve needed changes. At this point in time, there appears to be a mixed set of results. In many cases technology has speeded processes and generated short cuts to eliminate old systems that were outdated, but removed the customer from his or her rightful place at the center of an enterprise. On the other hand, some people have become so overwhelmed by the amount and isolation of too much electronic communication, that they have become less effective in dealing with the emotions and attitudes of people at work, creating gaps in needed communication and connection. The answer lies not in less use of technology, but in more effective uses of technology married to more effective interpersonal and personal strategies which allow workers to engage with people more deeply when they meet or connect, whether it be by voice or some other electronic vehicles for communication. People need to use technology—not be used by it. Newer innovations of office sharing systems such as those being introduced by Microsoft in its next iteration of Office—the ubiquitous tool of the modern corporation—hopefully will produce more real opportunities for connection and collaboration without becoming simply another technology tool that puts more "distance" between the very people who desperately need to connect in deeper ways.

CHAPTER 4

Conclusion

There is no doubt that the world is a vastly different place than it was in 1950 or 1980—or even 2001. It continues to be shaped by political, social, cultural, and economic forces. People working in organizations are strongly influenced by these forces, and it is important to be aware of what is happening more broadly in society to understand the reactions and opinions of workers. Workers are also impacted strongly by the style and management/leadership approaches in organizations and the strategies and technology these organizations employ to stay viable. Continuing to monitor these broad trends is essential to being a professional in the fields of leadership, as well as personal organizational development.

In the 1995 book *In Over Our Heads: The Mental Demands of Modern Life*, Dr. Robert Kegan suggests that modern life and its expanding complexities is too difficult for the average person whose development is not at sufficient levels of conscious understanding. While we agree with Dr. Kegan that life is increasingly complex and that many may be stumbling to grasp how best to work at life and its expanding complications, our own research implies that many people are evolving or are evolved in ways that are helping them cope with complexity and change. People are being influenced by many of the trends and situations we have discussed to have higher levels of adaptation to change, greater emotional intelligence, and greater openness to engage with new ideas and approaches. This may be due not just to increasing exposure to more mature ways of thinking about life and work, but also due to the aftereffect of events like 9/11, which for many was an extreme experience requiring a new lens to view reality. We are encouraged by our findings that for the most part, many people we surveyed and talked to perceived that they had much of the "right stuff" to both cope with and manage change and complexity in their lives and at work. They welcomed the chance to adapt, grow, and reinvent themselves to cope with new conditions and did not, as a group, seem either afraid of change or worried about it.

Our work has given us sufficient evidence that success in organizations or in an individual life does not mean simply handling change, or responding to change. Rather, success with change means leading change, or creating the internal changes one needs to thrive in life, not just survive. Organizations as a whole are best off when they are innovating and carving out new markets and/or new and better strategies and approaches to customers and their markets rather than just fending off competition or floundering to cut costs to survive.

We best deal with change when we are aware of it and open to the good it brings while minimizing the negative it might be creating. We also deal best when we are in touch with ourselves and our own values as well as life's core unchanging principles so that we can grasp what is changing and leverage it to improve or expand our lives and those of our neighbors and colleagues. Finally, we need to be aware of what trend or change is dangerous so we can minimize its impact or deal with its aftermath.

We do well when we get out in front of the trends and evolutions that are continuingly reshaping our modern world. In many cases, we might never individually be able to see what the world is coming to—but collectively, through interacting with others, listening to multiple viewpoints, reading, and working diligently, we can often see ahead to what is coming and prepare for it. And once immersed in organizational life of any kind—our mosque, church, or synagogue, our place of paid work or volunteer group, our political party or local club—it is imperative that we become a continual part of the process of improving and shaping these institutions to be more adaptive, more creative, and more flexible. Growth is collective as well as individual. The more we grow personally, the more we grow collectively to create the world we want to create, not just suffer the aftermath of violence like 9/11 or corruption in its many forms.

We have learned a great deal by listening to our data. It is rich in its complexity. We are offering our interpretations of it to you so you can take our insights and combine them with all that you are seeing and experiencing in your own life in terms of change, adaptation, and growth. We hope to influence you to consider that despite the troubling world in which we live, there are many positive aspects to the ways in which individuals and organizations are evolving. While clearly not everyone benefits from every dramatic change, and some changes can create havoc and confusion, collectively it appears that more people benefit from evolutionary changes—as long as they develop the appropriate tools and skills to work well in multiple situations, and they approach change with an openness and flexibility. From where we sit, it appears that many more than we initially realized are doing just that.

PART II

Phase I Research: The Myth of Change Resistance

SYNOPSIS AND IMPLICATIONS

Phase one of our research involved about 315 subjects who responded to an open survey we developed and put on the Internet. We worked with an organization to help us get a spread of ages and a mix of sexes as well as some diversity in terms of race and background. We accomplished this and had a mixed sample. We also interviewed a number of people in depth after the survey was completed and analyzed the results to get additional insights into our research questions.

In phase one we were asking two major sets of questions. The first had to do with change in general and how people felt about it and dealt with it in all aspects of their lives. Secondly, we asked questions about 9/11 and living in a world of terrorism. Since we surveyed people all over the United States and some internationally, we did not see or account for any bias of people who were close to the events of 9/11. Some suggest that 9/11 was an event largely lived and felt on the east coast of the United States Our research did not support this contention with no differences found in our sample based purely on geography. Simply put, we were looking to learn what people's attitudes and feeling were about change and adaptation and how all this played out in relationship to living in a post 9/11 world.

The results were very strong, persuasive, and not ambivalent. Across all ages, sexes, races, and backgrounds, people were strongly pro-change, open and willing to change personally and professionally, if they were clear that change was needed in many situations in the world today and were aware that without change and often strong change they could not succeed personally or professionally. There were virtually no differences by group—a very unusual and different result than one might expect.

In terms of living in a terrorist world, clear patterns emerged. People have become much more self- involved and family-centric. One's home, family, personal life, and all things personal are more important than careers, money, or moving ahead. Health concerns took precedence over business opportunities. While not surprising to some, the findings certainly contained rich data for people running organizations or working in them. People want and expect different things from organizations—and their commitments to them are clearly less intense than when the world was a safer and more secure place, or at least perceived to be such.

The three chapters in Part II go through the details of all the questions asked in both parts of this portion of the research. It also shares specific data suggesting what small differences existed between various groups of those that responded. Portions of interviews with ten different people are also included which shed light on the feelings, needs, and concerns of a range of workers from their 20s to their early 60s who work in a variety of settings. This interview data helps support our recommendations later on as well as suggests that our data was accurate in the surveys.

This result we found—namely that people are very strongly pro-change and deeply impacted by the new world order—encouraged us to look further to see if, in fact, the differences in various organizations would influence how people specifically dealt with change and handled change in organizations—not just what they thought about change. We were surprised at the depth of the material and how different these views were from the commonsense wisdom of change resistance and the dismay people seem to indicate when faced with making changes. If truth be told, we were expecting more sophisticated views, but the depth of people's sophistication, and openness to new thoughts and actions, did strike us as a profound and critical paradigm shift.

CHAPTER 5

More Pro-Change than We Knew

Was 9/11 an event that fundamentally changed people, effecting them to be more open to change? Do people resist change and growth as much as many business leaders seem to think they do because of 9/11? Why is it that so many organizations of all types that need to respond to opportunities and challenges in the world do not make the changes needed in appropriate time frames? These are distinct and yet inter-related questions in a post 9/11 world.

9/11 was not just a political, religious, or personally devastating event. It was also an economic event that for years threw southern Manhattan and New York City a serious economic curve ball. Its severe "temporary" effect on many industries like airlines and travel continues to affect many businesses even today. Like all tragedies, there has been a silver lining for some businesses such as security and related industries that find themselves more busy dealing with the fallout of a more safety-conscious, fearful, and concerned public.

As change consultants who have worked in organizations attempting to create and sustain change process initiatives, it often seemed to us that people were never as change adverse as management thought. Employees did have fears and issues about how changes might affect them. Employees that we worked with were also rightly skeptical of how the change would work itself out, what it meant for them personally, and how any new twist on the wheel would work out after the dust settled. This might mean they were cautious or sensible, but they never seemed adverse to change per se.

When 9/11 occurred, its impact began to filter into our brains and nervous systems. The question of how this event would or could transform or strongly impact people kept recurring to us. Would the post 9/11 times be a unique opportunity to look at people in the workplace and actually observe how they were thinking about change and adaptation? Could we use the post 9/11 world as a way to gain insight into people's thinking about themselves—and about change—and thus help both individuals and organizations understand what was happening to people and their attitudes about middle- to large-scale change? These types of questions were the impetus for the first part of our research.

After a number of false starts and with a good deal of help from colleagues, we finally developed an online questionnaire and let the pros do the job of getting a diverse audience to take the survey. We did not want the respondents to be people we knew or who worked in companies that might be current or former clients. The questionnaire was anonymous, although simple demographic data was gathered. Over 315 people from around the world and the United States responded to our survey; in addition, personal one-to-one in-depth interviews were conducted with a select group of people which honed in on reactions to 9/11 and thoughts about change. This first survey and interview phase of the research was completed by 2003.

This chapter describes the first part of the research—it looks at the survey itself, the questions asked, and how the participants responded. It also shares selected insights from the interviews—using disguised names and situations to protect the identities of those interviewed.

Table I describes the age and gender demographics of the participants who responded to the survey.

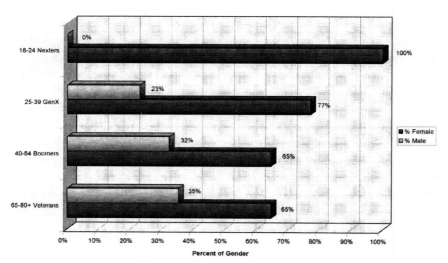

Table 1. Gender by Age Group

The survey was tested with many individuals to make certain it was easy to read and understand, but it has not been used beyond this research. The questions fell into two broad areas. The first set of questions, numbers one to ten, focused on what individuals thought about personal and organizational change, with no mention of 9/11:

Table 2. General Questions Regarding Personal and Organizational Change

I. People can change and often do change for the better.

2. People are who they are—with or without major drugs, therapy, or other intervention, they tend to stay the same.
3. I don't believe I need to change—and most people don't either.
4. I am always working to improve myself.
5. I let people and events affect me—not all the time, but when it matters.
6. I am my own person—things outside myself don't affect me all that much.
7. I think things happen for a reason—no matter what.
8. Changing, growing, being different is a good thing—things change and people change, and individuals and organizations have to respond to those changes.
9. If you don't believe in change and growth you are going to have a bad time in life.
10. If too many things outside of themselves influence an organization, country, or person, they lose their uniqueness and core roots and purpose.

When you look at the responses, the answers nearly "pop out" with strong majorities in each case, demonstrating people's significant pro-change choices.

Table 3. Responses to General Questions on Change

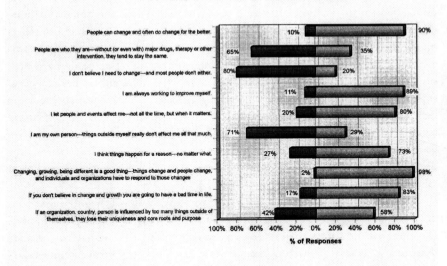

Our analysis of the results of these first ten questions follows. First, rather than being change-adverse, the vast majority of the respondents describe themselves as pro-change, open to personal development, and well aware that if they don't change with the trends and the times, they will suffer consequences. Second, the majority of people believe that individuals can and do change, and that change is possible and probable. Third, people believe that they personally, and their organizations, need to change to meet evolving conditions in the world. Fourth, people believe their needs to be a balance between adapting and keeping a core that remains constant. This last finding was the least supported.

These results were both tremendously interesting, positive, and in some ways surprising. Leaders in organizations nearly always start interventions in organizations with assumptions, often loudly expressing that "our people don't like change" or "we are getting lots of resistance" to the new initiative or new strategy. Or, "our people don't seem to get it," which is the leadership's way of describing the inaccurate perceptions of the current facts of their own organization's dilemmas, difficult industry trends, competition, or other "reality" faced by the organization. Could it be that our sample was a pure aberration and that people really *don't* accept the need for change? Or, could it be that people who answer online questionnaires are more pro-change than the general working population? Or perhaps people *say* they like and accept the need for change in their lives but in reality don't? Or, could it be that folks may understand change generically, but when faced with a crisis or situation "close to home," they miss it?

All of these are possible, and of course we don't really know for certain. But on the face of it, in direct questions, people do seem to come down clearly on the side of openness to change. This suggested to us, as we continued to reflect on the data and read the transcripts of interviews, that there might be something else going on. It would appear that some intermittent situation could be at play, something happening between the mindset, belief system, and values of people supportive of pro-change, and their seeming lack of enthusiasm for concrete and real change initiatives that they must adapt to and embrace at work. Or, of course an alternative view might be that the people in organizations do "get it," they do want to participate in constructive and positive changes, but the leadership of the organization is so used to assuming the opposite that the employees' behavior matches the employers' low expectations.

It was post this survey, and in tandem with the results of the interviews conducted, that we began to describe the findings as "the myth of change resistance." It seems that the data was so strong and so compelling that we had to conclude that there is, in fact, a "myth of change resistance." There is a real disconnect between what is going on with people and how they are being perceived and perhaps behaving. We further began to consider that the issue might be that people are more pro-change, but that getting close enough and in contact with employees is preventing leaders and consultants from understanding the true feelings and evolved thinking of workers.

These are conjectures, but we share them with you to challenge the thinking and assumptions of those who persist in believing that people are adverse to change. In the final chapter of the book we discuss implications of our research. Confronting people's assumptions about how others resist change will be addressed in that section as well. If our research is even partially valid, it is certainly the case that organizational leaders are operating with flawed assumptions that could lead them to make poor decisions in engaging staff in the processes of change.

One final explanation of why some sense change-resistance when, in fact, people are pro-change, might well be that people are adverse to the ways in which change is presented and expected in organizational life. Rather than people being adverse to change, they are often opposed to the means utilized, or strategies initiated to gain their involvement, incorporate their thinking, or expect to see results.

There were some differences to our change questions by age and gender. These might shed some additional light onto our discussion of the "myth of change resistance." For while it is clear that most people are strongly pro-change, some nuances and differences remain in how people view and accept change.

There has been much written about the age issues in organizational life. At the current time, the workplace is primarily made up of four distinct age groups—the Boomers and Xers are the largest, and the Veterans and the Nexters exert a strong impact on the workplace itself even though they are smaller. There are some consultants who contend that mixed-age cohorts at work is one of the most important challenges to consider in any organizational analysis, and when considering how change, other initiatives, or cultural shifts are viewed and handled.

In considering these differences, we decided to group and use a commonly understood construct. We grouped our age categories into those categories suggested by Ron Zemke in his book *Generations at Work: Managing the Clash of Veterans, Boomers, Xers, and Nexters in Your Workplace* (1999). While there exists some differences in how demographic experts and social science experts line up the four groups, this framework seems to be convenient (and well thought through) for understanding how people at work see themselves and sort themselves into broad categories. Zemke organizes the four groups as: Veterans (could also be known as Traditionalists, born roughly 1922-43); Boomers (born roughly 1943-60); Generation Xers (born roughly 1960-80); and finally Nexters (also known as Millennials, Gen Y or Echo Boomers, born since 1980). We would like to suggest that if the reader is not familiar with any of the literature in this area, they consider reading some of the most well-known books that illuminate this topic. We recommend the Generations book mentioned above, as well as others such as: *When Generations Collide: Who They Are. Why They Clash. How to Solve the Generational Puzzle at Work* (Lancaster, Stillman, 2002); *Human Resources in the 21st Century*, (Effron, Gandossy, Goldsmith, 2003); and *Connecting Generations: The Sourcebook for a New Workplace* (Raines, 2003). These and other books are listed in our bibliography for easy reference.

We will briefly consider some broad generalizations of each work group, and then indicate how these four groups handled our questions one to ten regarding change. This will be followed by a brief commentary. First, let's discuss the Veterans or Traditionalists. The Veterans were born and raised in the post WWII time frame. They were raised to be loyal and expect loyalty in return. Many worked for only one company or organization for much of their lives. This is a group of people who grew up with little resources so tend to be frugal and do not understand the need for debt—personally or at work. At work they do their jobs, take orders well, and accept the chain of command. Veterans tend to see those that don't obey the rules or don't work hard as "slackers." Although willing to work hard, they do not have the same compulsion to work as Boomers. They also respect positional power.

The Baby boomers—that pig in the python in the population picture—is next. These men and women, born into relative affluence and peaceful times, are currently in the majority of leadership and management positions as well as the most senior players in technology, professional services, and nearly any job category imaginable. This group is starting to retire or attempting to work part-time, as was previously addressed in the "Big Picture" section of the book. This group, known to be more socially liberal and democratic as well as hard-working and work-focused, will be leaving the workforce in the coming years. We know from studies that this group will not have similar retirements as their parents who were often retired to the Sun Belt with a focus on leisure. Either due to a lack of resources, or a desire to stay active and involved, today's boomers are likely to remain at least part-time in the workforce in relatively large numbers.

Many Boomers grew up with little (their parents were frugal, remember) and so pledged to give their children more than they had. In general, many left home by 18 and had to struggle to make ends meet. They grew up with a focus on work, work, and more work. They often put work and career first in their lives. Boomers tend to crave status and positional power. They are often the group most engaged with politics at work while their other cohorts just don't bother as much (Xers and Millenials especially don't get involved). Boomers are people focused as well on others (they brought us the civil rights movement, the women's movement, and so on), and think people skills should be a priority at work. They seek consensus and involvement.

Generation X, the more traditional and much smaller demographic born between 1960 and 1980 (again, in different texts the ages may be slightly different), are coming into power positions and demonstrating the first shift to wanting a more balanced life. Most GenXers have Boomer parents though some have

Veteran parents. While Veterans trust hierarchy, and Boomers want consensus, Xers value competence. They saw how the sacrifices of their parents at work often failed; they saw them laid off even after dedicating themselves to their careers. This led many to see life and "having a life" as more important than being totally work focused. They have a philosophy of fun, making a buck, and enjoying life.

Xers see Boomers as workaholics and too intense. They also see many of them as clueless about technology and the future, and as too personally "needy." GenXers, on the other hand, are often viewed by Boomers and Veterans as slackers, whiners, rude, lacking in loyalty, and uncommitted. GenXers are not as interested in positional power or traditional ways of doing things, and are in many ways "change masters." They grew up with change in every area of their lives and appear, for the most part, to expect it.

Finally, the Nexters, GenY, or Echo boomers, are the children of the Boomers, born starting around 1978. They are more inclined to want balance in their lives, be extremely comfortable with technology, and more liberal politically than the Xers. Generation Y was a wanted group of children raised by soccer Moms and involved Dads. They are the most creative generation in a long time and seem to always be asking WHY. They want to work in ways that allow them to be creative and to contribute. They get bored rather quickly with things and expect change and multiple jobs. They are highly adaptive with technology and want control over their lives and working conditions. Ys are the best at dealing with diversity of all types, communicating easily across racial and geographic lines via their cell phones and computers. They are also the most comfortable with a mix of men and women in the workplace. They are well-suited to the new global world of business that will make working with diverse groups and working digitally a common occurrence. They are by nature collaborators, thinking that people are important; they share this belief with the Veterans and Boomers, all of whom view the Xers as lacking in effective people skills.

Table 4a. Responses to General Questions 1-5 by Ages

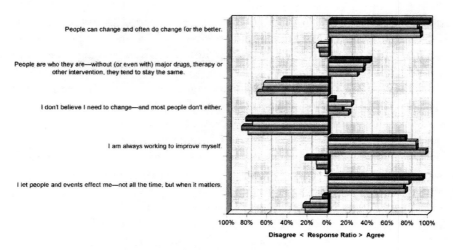

Table 4b. Responses to General Questions 6-10 by Ages

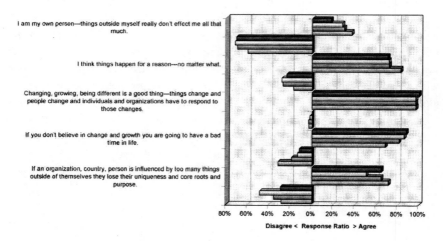

Interestingly, our Veterans are out in front with a pro-change approach. Although clearly all four groups were strongly pro-change with consistent answers in this regard—and in all questions—the Veterans showed most strongly in more questions such as "people can change and often do change for the better." Maybe they have lived long enough to see that in action. However, then they turned around and said people do tend to stay the same; this could be a contradiction or not. Veterans also thought they needed to change in greater numbers than the Boomers, Xers, or Ys. They were also more willing to be influenced by other external forces, with a larger percent agreeing that "I let people and events effect me—not all the time, but when it matters."

Our Ys didn't yet have the experience to see that if you didn't change in response to life circumstances, you would suffer. They disagreed in the largest amount to that question. But Ys led in the question about self-development; they saw themselves as continually working on themselves in greater numbers than others. This is logical since many are still in school part-time or full-time and hence continually in a learning mode versus a less constant learning mode for older groups.

Some might think the young are the most open to change, and even descriptions of groups we just provided, based on research about generational differences, suggest that X and Y folks are more change-oriented than their elders. However, our research did not support that. Question by question, the older groups were as pro-change and willing to change as the younger ones. When asked to agree or disagree that they are influenced by outside forces, the Ys disagreed more than other groups. They were more philosophical, believing "that things happen for a reason no matter what." Is that the optimism of the young or the realism of the older generations? We cannot be sure, but we do know our generational groups did not vary much in their pro-change approach, and when they did, it seemed our Veterans, Boomers, and Xers were all more pro-change, even if by small margins, than our youngest group of participants.

What about gender differences? Women are often thought to be more open to change; they seem more likely to go to therapy, talk about their lives, and implement personal self-improvement strategies. Even a cursory reading of male-oriented versus female-oriented magazines, web sites, and TV programs leave little doubt that women are more concerned with and focused on "fixing themselves," "improving themselves," or "reinventing themselves." However, men as well are gaining ground in their self-awareness and are increasingly participating actively in programs and interventions that are based on self-reflection and self-analysis.

In discussing the Big Picture, we spoke a bit about trends in leadership and workplace education. Mentioned briefly, Daniel Goleman's seminal work, *Working with Emotional Intelligence* (1998), brought the issues of self-awareness and self-regulation front and center in the organization. Self-help gurus of the last 10 to 20 years, from Tony Robbins to Dr. Deepak Chopra, have also added millions of men into the camp of taking stock and measuring up. And though Dr. Phil and other popular TV personalities may still attract more women than men, men are no longer a rarity in wanting to improve themselves and seek help with issues once considered odd, too "feminine," or unmanly. Further tapping into our Big

Picture is the whole diet, exercise, health, and spirituality movement, all of which brought millions of men from Neanderthal to metro guys. This created space for more self-reflection and brought the idea of "working on oneself" into the mainstream of modern life. Our research suggests that these cultural and work exposures to the issues of self-development helped to make our male participants almost as pro-change as our women. And as time progresses, that gap will continue to narrow.

Perhaps less likely to talk about change, men as well as women seem to have been influenced by the broader trends toward self-development and self-improvement. The phenomenon of helping oneself and pulling oneself up to be more than one's history or past is strong in our culture, and likely has strongly influenced both the sexes in this regard.

Table 5a. Responses to General Questions 1-5 on Change by Gender

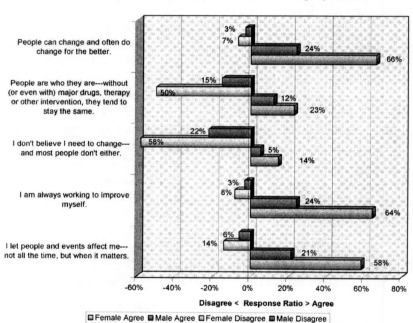

Table 5b. Responses to General Questions 6-10 on Change by Gender

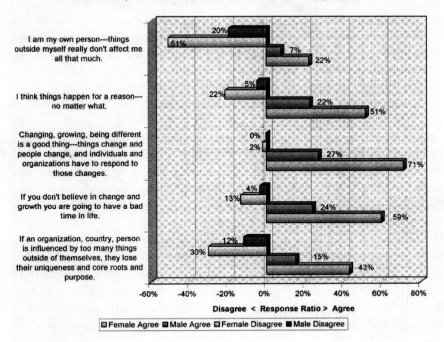

These tables need some brief explanation. For each question, all responses equal 100%. Since larger numbers of women answered our survey (roughly two-thirds were women), female percentages are always much greater. But if you look at the male totals being all male agree and disagree, and the female totals as female agree and disagree, you will get a clearer idea of how both men and women responded to change questions.

Although women appear on the surface to be more pro-change, once again we find very little difference in the number of men versus the number of women who were pro-change in any given question. For example, "I don't believe I need to change—and most people don't either." With 27% of the respondents being men, they agreed and disagreed in virtually the same ratio as did women who had 73% of the responses. Men also strongly agreed with, "I am always working to improve myself" again in similar ratios as women. And in the question, "changing, growing, being different is a good thing...", 100% of the men answered in the positive. Once again, our traditional views about who is and is not pro-change were challenged. In our survey, as with age groups, we found very little difference between how men and women answered questions about change and their willingness to embrace change.

"Changing, growing, being different is a good thing. Things change and people change and individuals and organizations have to respond to those changes." An overwhelming 97% of respondents agree with this statement. And yet, despite this, as stated earlier, we know that many people in organizations seem to give the impression of just the opposite view. What else did our research uncover that might further illuminate the disconnect between people's perceptions of being pro-change and organizations struggling to create change?

Let's meet Dana M., Larry H, Jim Y., and Mary S. Their names and some details of their stories have been changed to protect their privacy. Their stories might help clarify the issue of openness to change on the one hand, and the appearance of resistance or indifference to organizational change on the other.

Let's start with Dana. Dana is a young woman, under 30, working in New York for a major pharmaceutical corporation. She works in technology, having held a variety of jobs dealing with development of systems and systems security. She is sophisticated, knowledgeable, and hard-working. She is seen as a leader with a great career in front of her. When 9/11 happened, she was working and catching the news in bits and pieces, as were others in the company. Only after work did she realize the full dimension of the situation. In conversation with Dana, it became clear that although she felt that 9/11 was a big event that effected many people, she did not necessarily feel it was that major a change factor in her own, or in many of her peers' lives. She felt that increased interest in the news and patriotism were short-lived, and that most folks returned pretty quickly to life as they knew it.

Dana was very upset by the racism and anti-Muslim feelings expressed by many at work after the 9/11 tragedies. She admitted being shocked by the raw feelings expressed at work by some who saw the 9/11 situation as one pitting Muslims against Christians. She dismissed this analysis entirely, thinking that the reason for this incident related to foreign policy and perceived injustices felt by others around the world toward our systems, as well as our perceived arrogance and evil ways. She discussed her interest in history and her dream of someday getting a doctorate and becoming a history professor (despite her current career in information technology).

It was clear that Dana considered herself a citizen with a sophisticated view of world affairs. She also considered herself typical of her generation (Y, or Nextor, or Echo Boomer) that was both more cynical and more realistic than their boomer parents and bosses. While 9/11 was a terrible tragedy, many in her generation expected tough things to happen and tough times to exist. They were as shocked as other Americans by the events of 9/11, but Dana felt that many in her age group knew life was hard and that shocking experiences would happen. This might have been a different one than they expected, but loss and upset were part of their legacy.

Dana is not anti-change or anti-growth by any means. She talked about her desire to do more and earn more—to be more financially secure, and to perhaps someday be free to follow her dream of being a history professor. But would Dana be likely to be part of the group at work rallying around the latest change initiative? Likely no, if she did not perceive it as either important to the business as she understood it, or personally helpful for her and her work. Not a slacker or by any means resistant to new things, Dana is a realist and sees things going on around her with the eyes of someone who has already witnessed much in her relatively short life. She is not so much anti-change or change-adverse as she is focused on her own future, her work, and her life understanding that there is complexity all around and that simple rules don't apply. Dana would be the first to pitch in for a good cause or to help out. But without really knowing her depth of knowledge and interest in history and the roots of issues, she would likely not be easily led to consider any path not clearly presented in a way to gain her trust and influence.

Larry H. is a late forty something corporate executive from New Jersey. At the time of 9/11 Larry was working for a global drug company giant. Larry had worked there more than ten years and had a solid career in the technology and process improvement areas with opportunities for personal growth and responsibility. He long enjoyed his work, but 9/11 was a bit of a wake-up call to him on a number of levels.

Larry shared with Pat a number of serious and tragic events involving the early deaths of both his parents. He shared how the actual 9/11 event had a very profound affect on him for a number of days, arousing some reactions tied to these early losses. In the days following 9/11 he found himself reaching out to comfort others and even taking an international trip for business, but with a deep unease. The deep unease passed as he processed the event, but he later found himself considering if the time had come for new challenges that might be more aligned with who he had become over the years.

Larry shared that he found himself with some new and surprising interests post 9/11. While a voter, Larry never took much interest in politics but now found he was considering a more active involvement in state politics and his community. While always a reader and up-to-date on most current events, he discussed his new appreciation for the difficulties in the Middle East and new perspectives on world events. He also noted that his desire to travel and commute long distances from home also diminished, and he found himself considering new opportunities that would involve little travel and more opportunity to do meaningful work close to home.

Larry was open, trying new things and doing some deep reflection not just as a result of 9/11, but because the events of 9/11 created a space for him to think more deeply about what was important to him in his life and in his work.

Larry found himself more keenly alert to life, more aware of things and people around him, and yearning for more meaning in his day-to-day work.

While having a successful career, Larry was not one to have wished for or achieved a very high level of corporate success. He always did well, but his interest was the work itself—often related to process improvements—not getting ahead. And now, with the politics of the organization becoming more intense due to new regulation and reactions of senior management, and the changes planned not feeling that positive to him, he began to question what was next for him.

Larry and Pat spoke recently, a long time past his original interview. He appeared happy, relaxed, and very changed. He had left his corporate life behind and was now working at something he really enjoyed in the social work area. He also had gotten a new dog and was living a close-to-home life that he had first identified as critical post the 9/11 experience.

Jim Y. is a fifty something executive who took an opportunity to leave a county government position in a large county near Chicago that he had held for over fifteen years. He had worked in the government after he left the military in his late twenties and spent the bulk of his career moving up the ladder in various areas of land use and real estate. He candidly told Pat that he felt it was just time to go, that he had ceased to learn anything new, or to be challenged for quite some time, maybe seven or more years ago. He felt compelled to move on in his life.

In talking about the legacy of 9/11, Jim felt that although it was a tremendous tragedy, he did not feel his own life had been impacted much by the incident other than to worry that the country would go too far in the direction of eroding our own internal rights in what he felt was a flawed attempt to make us safer and more secure.

Jim was finding himself at a crossroads in his life. No longer challenged or learning at his job, and no longer needing it in the same way as when he was younger, he felt a spiritual pull to the ministry and was about to enter a two-year program to become an interfaith minister when he and Pat spoke. He thought it would give him an opportunity to expand his horizons and move beyond the work experiences he had had and the wonderful career that he enjoyed for many years.

Jim is the type of person who always sets goals for himself and achieves them. A loyal worker for the government, he excelled at his work and was promoted a number of times in his career. He had been given increased responsibilities as long as they were available, and in addition taught part-time and held a variety of other roles, both personal and professional, while working full-time for the county government. If there was a challenge, Jim was ready to take it on. But at this point in his life and in his career, Jim felt internally pulled in new directions that made him not want to continue the status quo of his life and his work. No one could likely be more pro-change, pro-development, or interested in new challenges than Jim. But it would be surprising if Jim could be convinced to go back into any type of traditional job, or be committed to any new efforts at his job within the year prior to his leaving. He just wasn't *into* it anymore.

Mary S. lives in England and is in her late thirties. Married and a successful career woman without children, Mary spoke to Pat about her view of life post 9/11 and its impact on her life and career. She described the effects of 9/11 as pivotal for her. She felt it was a wake-up call for her to look at her own life. Her husband, who she described very lovingly, was ill for a time prior to the event. His illness coupled with the 9/11 tragedy persuaded Mary to evaluate how she was spending her time. She had started a business a number of years earlier and was extremely successful, but she was busy all the time. She began to see that what she really needed to do was wind down her business and start a new path that would create more balance and time in her life.

Mary talked about how she became more internally driven as she aged. Rather than being pulled and pushed by things around her, she listened more now to her heart and spirit. She found, through a series of efforts, a wonderful new opportunity that would give her just what she wanted and needed professionally while keeping her time in balance to spend with family and friends. Mary shared with Pat details of her early life. Her folks had gotten divorced when she was quite young, and since she was the oldest of three children she "grew up fast." Mary felt it turned out to be a good thing for her since the divorce situation prepared her in life to be independent. She saw herself as a strong person, determined to succeed, and she did. The move to a different type of position was exciting because she felt it was the right fit for her spiritually, emotionally, and professionally. Mary struck Pat as a risk-taker and a woman who went for her dreams. But she demonstrated a strong inner core that would not likely be led in a direction that she did not feel was right for her or her career.

Mary S., Larry H., Jim Y., and Dana M. are "pro-change" people. They were open to new viewpoints, influenced or not by 9/11, and capable of being deeply committed to work and people in their lives. Their experiences indicated they were not stuck, not adverse to taking a new approach or to honoring their inner needs for something new. This is in sync with our findings about people being open to change. However—and this is a very big *however*—just because these folks are open to change and are willing to grow and be the best they can be doesn't mean that they would jump on the bandwagon to participate in or be a leader for workplace change. It seems that when one begins to dig deeper into people's newly more-developed selves, their reasons for being open to change, and the subsequent ways to engage them, become more complex.

There is no doubt that Dana, Larry, Mary, and Jim are winners who embrace life and change. They are thoughtful, sophisticated, and willing to connect with others. If they were approached with a deep respect and interest in their personal well-being, and an understanding that help was needed, all of them would respond to organizational efforts at change. But without that connection to their needs, aspirations, and sophisticated thinking, the latest corporate move or organizational realignment they were asked to participate in would not be of interest to any of them.

If organizational leaders and managers that are working with today's work-force cannot or will not be open to the individual and to connecting with them on issues that are important to them personally and individually, they could potentially miss the very momentum these people have to pursue change and growth. People have a great deal of passion. This passion can very often be utilized to steer organizations in important and necessary new directions. But there is the need for real connection, for recognition of people's issues, fears, joys, and priorities in order to advance change.

In an earlier part of the book we discussed the Big Picture, in which the issue of technology was covered. In many ways the advance of technology has limited the amount of one-on-one conversation and "deep knowledge" of others at work. While we communicate frequently and often by email and IM, the nature of that communicative interaction may not expose what is on their minds and what could engage them more fully at work, or for that matter at any organization in the community, from a Church to a foundation to a political club.

Unless you really know Jim, Larry, Mary, or Dana on a personal level, you might well miss all the passion that they are clearly capable of demonstrating. Just as we are missing opportunities to know individuals and what would bring out their personal best, we miss opportunities to capitalize on their teamwork potential as well. Teamwork is most effective when we tap into the genius of each person—their insights and creativity—but often that synergy doesn't come together at work because the scope of their interests, aspirations, and talents are not known.

In each of these interviews, we found people who were complex, multi-talented, and open to learning and changing, and in fact were making real changes in their own lives. The question is, would this talent have been picked up and utilized in a typical business culture? Probably not, and that is why the very creativity so needed by an organization is so often easily missed. Perhaps this discussion illuminates why people who happen to be very pro-change in their personal lives are not contributing at work in ways that leaders could recognize their pro-change attitude. Strategies to address this disconnect will be presented at the end of the book.

CHAPTER 6

9/11 and Other Change Levers

Returning to the first part of the research, the following questions followed the first ten and focused on 9/11, the emotional aftermath of the event, and how people respond to change as a result of other factors in their lives:

TABLE 6.

QUESTION 11. OVERALL REACTIONS TO 9/11 (check all that apply)

Our Pearl Harbor.

A terrible tragedy but sadly inevitable given our lifestyle and values.

A terrible tragedy that has fundamentally changed the American way of life.

A terrible tragedy that has changed some people and not changed others.

It caused me to wake up and make some real changes in my life.

It was a terrible thing of course, but it really didn't affect me that much.

I don't know what it means—but we should keep trying to figure that out and never forget.

Made me more patriotic.

Didn't affect my patriotic feelings one way or the other.

Think that in the long run, except for those directly affected by the loss, it might have been a good thing for this country to wake us up to global realities faced by others around the globe.

Think that in the long run things will go back to the way they were before 9/11—people forget history.

QUESTION 12. OVERALL REACTIONS TO 9/11 (Please enter others you would like to add)

QUESTION 13. FEELINGS DIRECTLY RELATED TO 9/11 (check all that apply)

My family is more important to me than ever.

My own time is as important as my time at work.

I am more spiritual.

I am less spiritual.

I am more focused on getting my own needs met while I can.

I am more fearful of flying.

I won't travel as much.

I have decided that I need to tell people in my life I love them and show more concern for them.

I am more anxious.

I believe we are now in a strange new world—and I don't like it.

I believe the world was always awful—we as Americans were just not having experiences others were having.

QUESTION 14. FEELINGS DIRECTLY RELATED TO 9/11 (Please enter others you would like to add)

QUESTION 15. OTHER SOURCES OF CHANGE—PUTTING 9/11 ASIDE (check all that apply)

I make changes in my life all the time—but the changes come from within me and are not based on things like 9/11.

There are events that have shaped my life—a unique and difficult job situation, my Dad's death, my folks' divorce...but they are personal—an event like 9/11 just would not tend to change me that much.

QUESTION 16. The top three influences that would cause me to make a change would most likely be related to something happening in these areas:

Family

Friends

Religion

Work/Career

My personal history—something came to light. I went to therapy and discovered something.

My politics

My health

My race or background

My motivation and drive to succeed

My age

My lifestyle, which I see as unique

Recent trauma (not 9/11-related)

Other

Now, let's consider how people responded to these questions directly related to 9/11 and to the other factors that might cause them to change or be more open to change.

Table 7a. Overall Reactions to 9/11

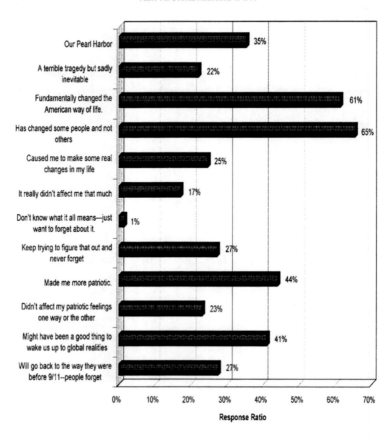

We can see that there were many interesting and strong feelings connected to 9/11. Fully 35% of people saw it as our Pearl Harbor. 61% felt it has changed the American way of life. That is further supported by the fact that only 27% of people thought that things would go back to "normal" or the way they were before 9/11. If you reflect back to Part I of this book and the commentary on terrorism, we note that this prediction of people closer to the actual events of 9/11 has come to pass. While 9/11 was traumatic at the time, it also definitely changed our way of life and continues to do so nearly four years post the event. From self-imposed travel restrictions to new needs for government spending, from new approaches (successful or not) to foreign policy to new anxieties that keep us more concerned about our safety and well-being than in previous years, America has changed and continues to change in reaction to terrorism on our own soil. While it is true that some post reactions, such as the feeling that we were "all one" or needing to treat each other with respect, may *not* have survived much beyond the first year, other changes in a post 9/11 world have remained and continue to evolve.

We felt it was significant that only 1% of people wanted to "forget" about 9/11. To us, this demonstrated maturity on the part of people who experienced 9/11. Rather than dwelling on events, people clearly choose to reflect on them and perhaps even to learn from them while attempting to integrate the meaning of this tragedy into their lives. Patriotism clearly increased post 9/11. In observing other cultural trends, we would have to conclude that this, too, is still the case nearly four years post 9/11, although not in exactly the same way patriotism was present in the months following the event. Continued and increased patriotism can be seen by the universal respect, acceptance, and support of our soldiers serving overseas. While agreement about the war in Iraq has been decidedly mixed, there is no evidence that Americans are anything but tremendously supportive of our troops and their heroic efforts in the face of armed and dangerous conflict.

Our research demonstrates that 9/11 was for some what learning theorists and experts might call a disorienting dilemma. In the adult learning field, Jack Mezirow developed a theory of adult learning that suggested that an important or critical event or personal trauma such as a divorce, going into the work place for the first time at an older age, getting fired, or any other number of personally perceived difficult or challenging events can trigger a dilemma for the person. They can cause a unique opportunity to learn, grow, and develop a more open and sophisticated perspective on an issue or set of issues related to the critical event. Through this transformative learning process of exploring and "trying on" new behaviors, a person has the potential to develop a more mature perspective through a process of analyzing and thinking through options that would make their new, changed life situation successful.

For example, a person going through a divorce might have had a certain vision of the world that suggested that to be happy one has to be married, or that divorce is a bad thing that destroys families and can limit success. Once the person begins the process of examining his or her life post the divorce, options and new ways of thinking and behavior begin to emerge. Transformed roles and adjusted ways of being are explored, tried and, hopefully, successfully adopted. This evolved way of thinking and being that a divorced person can experience can result in both happier and more fulfilled lives. This "adult learner"/divorced person now "sees" his or her life in a broader, more mature, open way with more options and ways of operating than before. He is transformed or could be said to have had a transformative learning experience that has led to more maturity in his thinking. This growth is not, of course, guaranteed, but with tragedy and change does come an opportunity for such growth.

When we experience a difficult challenge or perceive a new opportunity, we are usually more open to considering a changed perspective, approach, or model.

While it is true that tragedy prevents some people from fulfilling their dreams, there is an equally large volume of literature that suggests that resilience is a quality that many have and use in the face of challenge. In fact, we know that resilience is an important characteristic of people who are successful in life and at work.

9/11 was for many people a disorientating dilemma—a unique and distinct event serving as a catalyst for learning and growth. For those unfamiliar with this theory of development, the authors would suggest a fuller understanding of transformative learning. Here are a few options: Pat Cranton's *Understanding and Promoting Transformative Learning: A Gude for Educators and Adults* (1994) or *Fostering Critical Reflection in Adulthood: A Guide to Tranformative and Emancipatory Learning* (Mezirow, 1990). Karen Watkins, in her text *Facilitating Learning in the Workplace* (1991), provides a look at transformative learning in the workplace. These books and others in the bibliography will help establish more clarity on how adults learn and potentially develop both personally and in the workplace as a result of a triggering event. This is especially relevant for change agents whose work might, in fact, stimulate a disorientating dilemma for some at work, creating a unique opportunity for learning and development on the part of the workforce.

Returning to our post 9/11 data, the chart below shows how participants answered the question we posed about the tragedy.

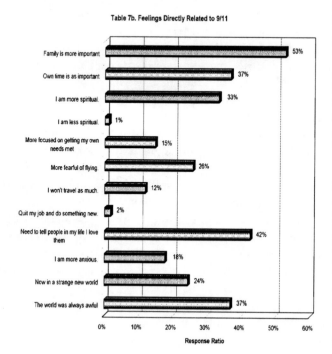

Table 7b. Feelings Directly Related to 9/11

Not surprisingly, we can easily observe that 9/11 took a toll. As with other studies post 9/11, our research was consistent in indicating stress and other negative impacts. Ninety percent of respondents from a large United States study reported at least one symptom of stress as a direct result of 9/11 (Shuster et. al., 2001). In addition, the popular literature was filled with all the negative effects of the 9/11 terrorist attacks (e.g., employees would spend less time at work, engage in greater ethnic and religious harassment, and have more negative job attitudes) (Boyle, 2001; Cole, 2001; Gibbs, 2001; Richards, 2001; SHRM/ee-Pulse, 2001).

When we look at responses to questions about the feelings of people post 9/11, we see clearly a tremendous amount of emotion, which is why the event (or the more recent 7/7/05) can be defined for many as a disorienting dilemma. We can see from the data that people reacted not just intellectually, but spiritually and emotionally as well. And it is clear that for some it did allow a certain amount of learning and growth to take place. The list of responses and the range of answers tells us that people are complex and react to events in complicated ways. These emotions were not put aside when they went to work—that would not make sense. People come to work as a whole person, even if they are not treated as such by the organizations for which they work. 9/11 provided a terrible and unique opportunity for most Americans to feel the danger, the panic, and the fear that sadly is part of the lives of so many others around the globe. For most of us, it was the only attack on our soil we have ever known. It was an event so startling, so unnerving, that it allowed many of us to get in touch with pieces of our hearts and souls that we had not previously touched. 9/11 did not change everyone, it did not even impact everyone, but for many it served a unique role in their lives. For organizations, this opportunity for deep understanding of their employees was often lost—not out of malice, but likely due to the real need for businesses to focus on their own requirements as business entities. This was unfortunate. For as the world has continued to change, this opportune time when people would have been most open to share with leaders what was on their minds and how they could best be engaged was missed. If we focus on those largest responses of our participants, we note that the desire to be closer to one's family and balance work and home life is one of the strongest feelings that developed as a result of 9/11. This is certainly a key point and one that has been noted in other research post 9/11. As mentioned earlier in the section on the various ages at work, Xers and Ys already possess a strong need for work and life balance. What we are seeing in this data is that for all age groups this need for work and life balance is being intensified as a result of 9/11.

But 9/11 impacted something else. It impacted ideas about the world as a global community. By referring back to the overall reactions to 9/11, we note an interesting question that received a 41% agreement. "Think that in the long run, except for those directly affected by loss, it might have been a good thing for this country to wake us up to global realities around the globe." We found it very intriguing that so many people agreed with this statement, confirming our intuition that for some the event was a trigger for deeper learning and reflection about the world at large and our relationships within that world. We noted an increased interest in and response to global politics and the results of our actions as a nation. In interviews we found that strong feelings about the global situation were held by a number of people, and some people actually changed gears and thinking about their path as a result of the event. Some of their comments and thinking struck us as both fascinating and worth reflecting on.

Let's consider some more stories—about Dan S., Donald Z., and Karlie M.—who were people with strong feelings about 9/11 and its aftermath. To some their stories may seem extreme, but to us they represented the wide range of reaction and opinion that is now part of the modern population of workers and citizens.

Dan S. is a fifty something computer expert who operates his own small business in Pennsylvania. He has an undergraduate and graduate degree and a successful business history. His wife is a flight attendant for a major air carrier. They live in a suburban area near Philadelphia. 9/11 brought a number of significant changes for Dan and Lisa. Lisa, of course, had a job that was instantly affected by 9/11. Dan, who had been working for another computer support company, got laid off shortly after 9/11 due to some down time that the business could not withstand given their small size. Dan and Lisa also had some friends and fellow church members die in the 9/11 tragedies.

Dan is an easygoing person. He has lived in several places around the country and has always worked in business settings, often with corporations. He is somewhat new to running his own business but has handled it in stride. Dan is not someone that is strident, hard to work with, or anything other than warm and pleasant. It was quite intriguing when we met for an interview that he held very strong and pronounced feelings about the postterrorism climate. Dan articulated that he felt the world was in a war between Muslims and Christians. He felt certain that the goal of many Muslims was actually to kill all infidels—those who are nonbelievers. He felt this was part of their deeply-held beliefs. And although not every Muslim may feel the need to act on this aspect of their faith, many clearly did.

Dan also voiced serious concerns as well about American society and culture, which he felt was going in the wrong direction. Although he did feel many Americans were deeply religious and many others were becoming more so, he thought a certain moral decay in the country was going to cause some long-term problems for the nation.

Whether one agrees or not with Dan, his beliefs are strong and deeply held. If one worked with Dan and did not know him well, one might think that he gave little thought to outside or global issues or that he might just "go along" since his demeanor is so calm and collected. One might also think that Dan was not the type to get worked up or deeply concerned about many things. But this is clearly not the case. Dan is a man with well thought out ideas and beliefs that influence the way he works, who follows through on commitments, and who handles disappointments and personal crisis. His beliefs influence his actions and behavior, and his moral center dictates both his operating principles and resulting behavior.

Donald Z. lives in Oklahoma. He is in his fifties, has lived in several parts of the country, and is currently the President of a medium-sized university. He has a doctorate in education and has traveled extensively around the world to over 70 countries. Donald was frustrated post 9/11. He saw the attention being paid to the tragedy as overblown and in error. He felt that although 9/11 was of course a horrible tragedy and a larger event than even the terrorists themselves imagined, it was only one of many ongoing and horrific tragedies going on daily around the world, such as poverty and the AIDS epidemic. He felt that 9/11 was a horrible event, but he resented the lack of attention being paid to other large and horrible events happening daily around the world. He says he is continually reading and absorbing news of world events mainly on the Internet, since he views the mainstream media as "out of touch" with global realities.

Donald considers himself more evolved and more of a global citizen than many in the United States. A modest and low-key man, Donald was not so much tooting his own horn, but rather suggesting that due to his extensive travels and wide network of friends and colleagues around the globe, his perspective on the events of 9/11 would be, of course, different than the average American who may have limited knowledge and experience outside of their own town much less their own country.

Donald was concerned about the Bush administrations' "black and white" thinking on a variety of issues that he thought in no small measure may have helped create the conditions for the 9/11 incident. He feared that the United States government would crack down and create a bit of a police-type state in the hysteria after the tragedy, not thinking of the tremendous problems such short-sighted acts would have. Since we haven't connected with Donald in awhile, we are unsure what he would think of the continuing Bush foreign policy including the Iraq war, but feel confident that he would not be pleased with the way things have progressed.

Donald did not see himself as particularly influenced by 9/11, and yet our conversation indicated that some different thinking and opportunities for conversation had some small impact on Donald and, if nothing else, had continued to affirm his position on world events and the need for a more sophisticated and nuanced foreign policy.

Donald is not a person to react violently or in any way that is extreme. Though his ideas and views might strike some as different or extreme, he is himself soft-spoken, confident that he could handle whatever goes on in the world, and thought about events somewhat dispassionately. Donald is, for lack of a better word, philosophical about life, change, and influence. He knows that injustices of all types exist, and that ignorance of all kinds is widespread. He is certain that his own work is helping in the world, but likely will be unable to change it much. And though disappointing for him, he is clear that this is the way of the world and he can only have so much impact.

Karlie M. is a thirty something northern California executive with a long history of senior positions in corporate life. She was working for a major media company at the time of 9/11. She described how 9/11 "changed everything for me." Apparently the devastation felt in N.Y. hit the west coast as well. Karlie shared how the whole company was traumatized for a long time, it was topic A for many for an extended period, and also woke her up to the realization that she did not have a family. She had always been so completely involved in her work and in her career. She was happy with her career—or so she thought, but when this event hit, the fact that she was essentially alone, without a partner and without children, made her feel for the first time that she really had to transform her life in a major way.

In addition to this wake up call, Karlie started taking better care of herself. She sought some medical help for anxiety and started taking medication that was making her feel whole, grounded, and in control for the first time in many years.

Karlie described the changes in her routine, from more time with friends, to increased boundaries at work. While late nights and weekend work was a common occurrence prior to 9/11, post the event Karlie started leaving the office promptly at 6:00 p.m., still committed but not as single-minded as in the past.

Karlie also talked about her renewed and increased interest in foreign affairs, politics, and the like. Formerly a bit detached from events such as those happening in the Middle East and Afghanistan, she now found herself reading more and getting more engaged with understanding the complexities of global events and attempting to figure out directions she thought the United States and other governments should be taking moving forward. This also helped her gain needed perspective in her own life. Where minor events would become traumas and part of the "Karlie drama show," the realization that there was a bigger and more complex world out there made Karlie a broader thinker and more aware of the complexity of events and their consequences around the globe.

She talked at length about the bravery of those involved in helping at the site of 9/11 and the tremendous generosity and outpouring of support for so many. Karlie was certain that much of what was happening close to 9/11 would have a long-lasting effect. She certainly hoped that many of the "positive" effects such as increased kindness would last. Perhaps it has, though that is hard to say.

For Karlie, 9/11 was not a result of religious belief or ideology. Unlike Dan S., she saw the reasons for 9/11 as related to our wealth and jealously over our material success. She did not feel that Muslims as a group were to blame and that unfortunately, since ignorance still exists, we may continue to be at risk in the future. For her, 9/11 was a wake-up call to transform her own life, to take more responsibility for going after what she wanted and deserves as a person, while continuing to work hard, be a more concerned citizen, and hopefully a better human being.

Clearly Dan, Donald, and Karlie represent a wide variety of views and a diversity of reaction to 9/11. Some, like Karlie, experienced a real change in perspective and were motivated to make serious and profound life changes that are still unfolding. Others, like Dan and Donald, may not have changed as much as continued their learning journeys and evolved their thinking about world events since these interviews took place. Reflecting on their stories and viewpoints, one cannot help but think that each of these people brings enormous passion to their lives and have the capacity for bringing deep passion to their work. But could any of these people be said to be "typical" or holding a simple viewpoint? Clearly no.

If these people are indicative of the broader population, we know that not only has 9/11 created shifting perspectives, those perspectives are neither simple nor consistent. People are thinking and reflecting on complex international as well as intra- and inter personal issues. They are thinking, considering, and engaging with themselves, others, and the society at large, contributing to a complicated conversation about where the world needs to proceed, and where our nation needs to proceed. They also are likely having a variety of discussions on how their own lives need to proceed, as well as their careers and the organizations they work for.

When considering how this affects openness to change personally and at work, this research found that simple assumptions about people cannot and will not work in understanding how to work effectively with them in any given work situation. People are engaged in new ways with the world and spending more time thinking about the world at large than previously. Certainly not all people have become more sophisticated or exploring, but we are likely to believe relatively large numbers have become more engaged.

To us, this implies that people in the workplace will be open to hearing of the need to change or even perceive the need to change earlier or at the same time that the management does. They can and do respond to global events, but they will not accept simple or pat answers that assume, incorrectly, that they are clueless. They are not clueless about events in the world, they are not closed to change and the need for new ideas, processes, and new directions. However, some are wary and do have opinions and prejudices about the reasons things are the way they are. Our interviews suggested a wide variety and variance in why people believed things. Our current workforce appears to want to understand situations more fully, have time to process and think about the reasons for things, and then proceed to be more fully engaged.

People do not see solutions in simple ways either. While Fox News or other media outlets try to make dramatic differences and simplistic left or right views palatable and mainstream, it appears to us that more people see things in gray and in ways that are less black and white and simplistic than presented. More people are open to deeper and multiple realities, both because of the broad-changing cultural and globalization trends, and because they have seen that solutions to the world's problems like 9/11 do not come easily or simply. The war in Iraq further intensifies feelings that black and white and simple linear answers to questions of change are not workable. Whether one is for or against the war is irrelevant; the news continues to present information that illuminates the complexity of changing situations there, creating more evidence to modern workers and citizens that no major change can be accomplished in quite the easy way it is presented.

Since the "answers," if there are any, to complex situations internationally seem to defy simple pat responses, our workforce and citizens are less likely to accept any attempts to make things too black and white and simplistic within organizations. The selection of the new pope, Benedict XVI, has already concerned many American Catholics. It appears that many of the faithful, although willing to listen to the new pontiff, are complex in their thinking and do not want simple answers to issues they deem critical to the Church and its future. While the majority are comfortable with dogma in areas like abortion, others are unwilling to accept pat answers or pronouncements on the priest shortage, women in the priesthood, or birth control. This would be aligned with our research data, which demonstrates complicated thinking and the holding of various positions in the people we interviewed.

What is the point of this analysis for organizational change at any level? Our research into the reactions of people we spoke with and surveyed indicate that with any change it is wise to expect a wide range of reactions, and accept that simple, pat answers and any straight-line approach to an end point selected by an elite few (rather than groups as a whole) is bound to fail. Understand that people's thinking due to many factors noted earlier in the Big Picture in many cases has evolved and is complex. Expect a range of emotions to any serious change, understand and accept too that the personal impact of change, not the change itself, is often the issue for any individual worker or leader. There will be various and different approaches, emotions, and solutions generated by such diverse people, and that is more than "ok" if they are considered in the process. More about this will be explored in the final chapter.

Turning to the final questions on change, we see in the table below that there are some key factors more important than others that create the need to change or react to change. Looking beyond 9/11 we can determine that other factors influence people to make changes.

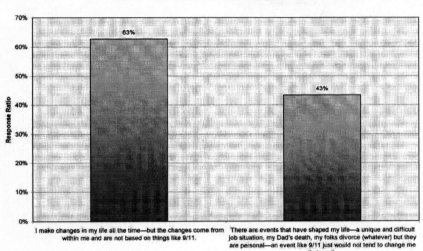

Table 8a. Other Sources Of Change--Putting 9/11 Aside

This table provides a visual of what people perceive to be going on within themselves, affecting their need to create change and to be open to change. We see a strong majority, 63%, indicating that they are making changes all the time in order to adapt to evolving conditions and new issues in their lives. 43% acknowledge that their own particular histories and their own reflections on life events are also impacting them and creating conditions for change. Once again our concept of "the myth of change resistance" appears to be valid. People appear to accept the need for change. But of course the issue for organizations is "what change" are they open to?

Organizations that do not allow for the understanding that most people appear to be changing all the time due to their own issues, miss the opportunity to engage with individuals to determine just how those specific changes that people are working on in their own lives might work for the common good or their own good at work. Leaders at all levels need to be aware that people are continually in flux, and that flux can work for or against any given change and/or issue at work.

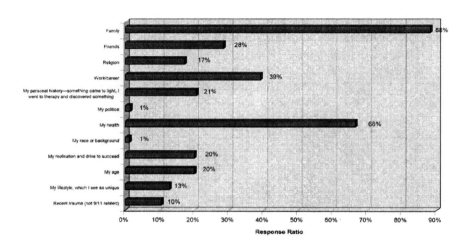

Table 8b. Top 3 Influences That Would Cause Me To Make A Change

This chart summarizes a critical piece of data relevant to organizational change. If you reflect on people's answers, strong messages emerge. Family is key, work and career is important, and health follows closely as triggers for change. These three variables account for the bulk of things that trigger personal change. It would follow then that people are most concerned with the micro picture— their world of family, work, and health. When organizational leaders do not address these, or consider their huge impact on people's willingness to act and how they act, they clearly will be unable to engage workers in meaningful change. In Covey's *The 8th Habit: From Effectiveness to Greatness* (2004), he makes the point that the key to success for organizations is to focus on the whole person—his or her mind, body, spirit, and core—not just his or her body or mind. Our research appears to support this contention. Our survey and interview data demonstrates that the whole person is who needs to be engaged if personal change is going to happen inside or outside any given work setting.

Let's meet Bob B., Kay R., and Natalie T. Their stories, again with disguised details, help illuminate the feelings of many who were impacted by 9/11 and need to be considered as whole people, not just workers, in a post 9/11 world.

Bob B. is a thirty something successful career executive from the New York area. He works for a major health corporation that is global in its reach. Bob is very outgoing, warm, and comes across as strong, purposeful, and on the top of his work game. Bob's wife worked in Tower One of the Trade Center for a major financial services company but shares a common story with other survivors that she didn't get to work on 9/11 due to an emergency involving Bob's job. She did see the first plane go in, and then the second, standing in horror on her commute that never finished. A late start saved her life and many others. Thankfully all but one of her coworkers lived. The one who did not was a hero who was making sure everyone else got out, and then waited too long to get out himself. Nancy, Bob's wife, worked in offices that were on a low floor for the towers (40), and most of those lost, of course, were on higher floors above where the planes went in.

Bob immediately made a point to say that he and Nancy had become a lot more family focused. They have three young children with whom they were spending more time by traveling less and working at home more for their busy careers. Still very committed to his career, Bob was strongly impacted to get back to what he and his wife felt was their first priority—their family and its well being.

Bob talked about how he did not think it was possible that the government could have put all the pieces together. As a worker in a large global enterprise, he spoke supportively of government workers since he shared the experience of working in a huge organization and well understood the difficulties of staying connected and working seamlessly keeping each other informed and in the loop. Connecting dots is a great deal easier on paper and in hindsight than it is within the confines of a real organization.

Bob felt he was a better father as a result of 9/11. While he was always a concerned and involved parent, there was now more of an emphasis on sharing and communicating. At dinner, Bob was asking questions about each of the children's days and how they thought about issues they were experiencing. He felt this was a great improvement in family life and was bringing them more together into a stronger unit that really understood each other's challenges. Because Bob's children were young, he also felt he had to answer their questions in a way that would help them begin to understand the world. Why do people kill people of different religions Daddy? (Some small numbers of people do this—not all.) Are we safe at the airport? (Yes, there is more security now.) Will you and Mommy be OK if you go on a business trip? (Yes, we will be OK.) These were new issues for he and his wife to deal with and they were dealing with them head on, trying to give their youngsters a sense of safety and an understanding that there were good people in the world—that, in fact, most people were good.

As for his job and career, Bob saw a bit of a pull back. He loved his work, but often an exciting new job opportunity would mean more trips to London, Singapore, or India, and Bob now felt that he didn't want to travel away from his family. He also knew that less travel meant less visibility in his corporation. He still wanted the successful career he was having, but he was going to make choices that likely would limit some options at a later time. He was at peace with that because he saw it as his own choice.

Bob also mentioned his father-in-law's death as a key event in his decision making around his own career. In Bob's mind, his father-in-law had a good career—he worked like crazy, put four children through college, and really focused on taking care of his family. Although he had hoped that his retirement would turn the tables a bit with him enjoying life more, he died, at his desk, of a massive heart attack at age 54. This, too, was part of the personal history that shaped Bob's thinking about the limits of his career ambitions, especially in light of events like 9/11.

Kay R. is an early forties insurance executive working in HR for a large insurance company in Ohio. She is married with twins and a working husband. Her husband is going to retire to spend more time with their children—not as a direct result of 9/11 but as one of many things that Kay felt was a result of thinking about the importance of family in a post 9/11 world. She is hard-working, very strong, and passionate about learning and educating adults at work; this is her area of expertise and she does it well. Kay puts in long hours and considers herself a real professional.

Kay described herself and her husband as conservative. She was spending a great deal of time helping her children understand the events of 9/11 which she saw as a seminal event in our nation's history. She was worried that time would make people forget the impact of 9/11; she thought this would be a loss. She was collecting many mementos and other items she felt would help her children remember and understand the complex situation that occurred. Kay felt patriotism for many had increased and she hoped this would continue. She felt confident that the United States would overcome problems and continue to be the best place in the world to live. She was one of the strongest people we interviewed in terms of her pro-America, pro-American way of life.

Kay was upset when one of her boys saw a middle-eastern man on TV and asked her "are they all bad Mom?" She worried that she and her husband's patriotism or conversation may have led her children to have prejudices or hold stereotypes. She confronted this directly with her son and assured him that no, not all middle eastern people, or even a majority of these people, were bad.

Kay found herself more worried than she would like over travel. She changed some of her travel plans due to her fears, which she hoped would subside with time. Kay thought a big change for her was an increased interest in all things political and in world events. As noted in discussions of earlier interviews, she felt she was becoming and had become more aware of and interested in world events. She felt concerned about the issues in the Middle East and voiced her belief that people in that area of the world seemed to have less concern for human life and the sacred nature of any life. While she didn't want to be negative and stereotype people, she felt there was something to the idea that certain people did not seem to care enough about life and that this created an opportunity for more terrorism in the world.

Kay felt that work also had changed due to 9/11. New economic forces were impacting their insurance business. She felt that the organization she worked for was putting an increased emphasis on helping people see the interconnectedness of events. If businesses lost ground, that would affect their own business since less people would or could pay for insurance. She felt that many, including herself, were becoming more realistic and clear that businesses were constantly dealing with change—and that employees needed to change alongside them. This is very much in line with our earlier observations that people are realizing the need for change. It appeared from her conversation that this new realism, if you will, was being nurtured at her organization, which certainly would be helpful for all workers there. Kay wants to continue to be successful and contribute at work. She is open to new ways of doing that and is anxious to continue being both a better and a more engaged parent, spending as much time as possible with her family and engaging with them in ways to continue to understand the new world in which we all live.

Natalie T. is a late forties corporate employee living and working in New Jersey with one grown daughter, a younger son, and a working spouse. Natalie has always worked although she cut back to part-time a few years ago to balance her work-life mix. She was visiting her mother in the hospital when 9/11 happened. She remembers calling her husband to go get her son and bring him home. It was a scary time.

Natalie sees herself as always having been family-oriented and patriotic. Her Dad was in the service and she grew up in a home that always flew the flag and believed in God, family, and country. She did not see herself as becoming more patriotic or family-oriented due to 9/11 because she always felt those were her priorities. But she did find herself believing that "life is short," and began to pick up old friendships and relationships she had neglected, calling friends she hadn't talked to in years and spending time with a broader range of people than before.

Natalie, like others we spoke with, was more interested than ever in the news and world events. She found herself for the first time very interested in global political issues and having conversations with people about those issues.

Natalie comes across as a very loving person. She mentioned that she had become more so and more spiritual as well. She felt enormous empathy for those who had died or had suffered the loss of a loved one. She felt that changes in her life were often related to personal events like her own divorce and the sadness she felt when it was happening. She saw that 9/11 had impacted many to share their own feelings that life was short and that family and friends always needed to come first.

She noted something quite interesting in her interview which focused primarily on her family. She talked about her passion for her work, and how at one time no one would have thought that "sweet Natalie" could have handled a job that had so much pressure and the need to make presentation all the time. Natalie expressed great pride in her accomplishments at work and felt this was an important part of her life. Natalie, for all her family focus, had passion for her career and work.

Bob, Kay, and Natalie are unique and yet represent some broadly held approaches and beliefs. They embody the spirit of many working people. They care about their work, but they care first and foremost about their family, their personal need to contribute in ways that make sense to them and use their skills, and about being healthy and being whole. Their stories are ones that put meat on the bones of the survey, which suggests that people are deeply and fully committed to change in their lives. But that is the key—in their lives. They are open to changes and opportunities at work. They are realistic about the needs for change in a global world. But people are not going to sacrifice their families' well-being, or their own well-being, just to respond to something that will likely change again at work. Work and workplaces need to tap into the need to contribute and be a whole person. If work allows people to do that—to achieve their personal dreams and aspirations and those of their families—then people are willing and able to go beyond any norms and contribute to make that happen. When the employee is made to feel that the organization sees them only in terms of their own needs, they disconnect and become unengaged with the real work of the enterprise, except as it meets their needs for money and survival. It is not surprising that they will avoid or be neutral toward active participation or a willingness to participate in transformation initiatives or change programs that the organization is undertaking.

CHAPTER 7

Conclusion

The first phase of our research was exciting and demonstrated, in our population of survey participants and interviews, that for the vast majority of people, change is good, acceptable, and part of their lives. They are moving toward change, not away from it. This held true for men as well as women and people in all age groups. Our research shows very little difference between those groups in terms of their attitudes toward and about change.

9/11 was a critical event in our history. It also served as a change stimulus for some and created opportunities for reflection and new directions in thinking. 9/11 seemed to allow for new conversations and ways of understanding the world that contributed to the open mindedness of many people.

We know for certain that family is more important to more people than ever before. But careers and health are critical too. People make decisions and change gears often. And the reason for these adjustments are often tied to that constellation of issues—family, career, and health.

Transformation is happening to some people—whether as a result of 9/11, other changes in the world, or personally. Some people are able to take on new perspectives and shifting beliefs that are strengthening them in their understanding of themselves and others.

Work is ever-changing. How workers react and respond to those changes is complex. But it is certain that workers are not adverse in this time in history to consider changing for work or at work. The question is how best to connect to more sophisticated and informed people who have their own eyes on their own priorities and are aware of the limitations of organizations to provide them with security of any kind. People want engagement and meaning, but it also appears from our look at modern organizations that they or their leaders are not quite sure how to go about providing connection and opportunity to achieve people's best work in this constantly changing world.

PART III

Phase II of Research: A Closer Look at Attitudes and Behaviors Related to Change at Work

SYNOPSIS AND IMPLICATIONS

We already knew by the end of the first phase of research coupled with our review of the culture and the times that leadership needed to change and that individuals were being under-estimated in terms of their sophistication about change. We also knew that there appeared to be less differences among people regarding issues of change as well as issues of family focus. While our industry had literature exploring differences among groups—and we don't dispute there are such differences between Baby boomers and Generation X for example, when it comes to change, and handling it, the differences did not surface in our research sample. This is an important finding in light of some organizations' out-of-date beliefs that one or another group may be more pro-change than others, or that younger people manage or deal with change more effectively—this simply did not hold true in our research. What about when you factor in differences in organizations? What about when management or leadership is doing a particularly good or poor job of managing and leading change efforts? How does that impact people and how do people, in a real and concrete way not just THINK about change, but behave when faced with real changes at work. We decided we needed a bigger sample of people and we needed to see them in specific contexts. We worked with about 640 people in this phase of our research and we honed in on reactions to tangible work changes and to behaviors when faced with complexity and change at work. We also continued to look for differences by age and gender. We surveyed people at all levels by education and title/organizational status. We did not tease out this data to look at differences, but if our data is consistent, it is likely not going to show many if any changes. Simply put, we did not see many differences between various types of people within any given organizations although some differences did emerge by organization.

We decided to do a couple of things in this phase of the research. First, after much effort, we selected eight specific work locations and a group of change consultants to study in more detail. For each we studied the industry, the organization, and the issues of change and how they were handled. Then, we grouped the sites into one set of four that were, according to our expertise and the literature of change more effectively handling change and leading the processes effectively. Then, we chose four sites which, for reason or another, in our professional judgment were not doing something right—either the leadership effort was off base, or the industry was going through some things that were troubling, or for some reason it just seemed things probably would not be going as well as planned.

In all cases we selected and used two validated and existing tools that research shows demonstrate two sets of things—the first tool measured people's attitudes and approaches to specific work changes—they were either for them, against them, or neutral toward them. Then we looked at another tool widely considered in business—emotional intelligence—and we measured how emotionally intelligent people were in these settings. This we measured in terms of how well they handled issues related to change—not just what they thought, but how they acted and if they demonstrated flexibility and good relationship skills that would help them navigate change effectively.

In the four chapters that follow we share the details of the sample, the tools used, the questions covered, and the various ages and gender mixes in addition to highlighting the stories of our sites and the analysis of where people are in terms of adaptation and behavioral approaches to change. Broadly, we discovered that the findings from the first phase which showed little to no differences between and among groups by age and sex carried through to this stage of the research as well.

Next we found, that although there were some minor and interesting differences among successful and less successful organizations, and there was variation in response patterns, for the most part people were both more emotionally intelligent and more pro-change than neutral or negative toward change.

The stories of the organizations—a brokerage firm, a global healthcare giant, a technology company serving the animal care industry, a large government agency serving millions of customers with thousands of employees, a large state government group that ran a well regarded court system, an entrepreneurial firm with high technology products for the visually impaired, an aviation company that serves unique niches in the marketplace, and a company doing outsourcing of communications for leading firms, are interesting and rich. They serve to demonstrate the range of organizations we considered and the range of workers and industries. In addition to these sites, we worked with a group of independent consultants specializing in organizational change and an additional 250 people who completed questionnaires and were from other industries and at a variety of levels within organizations than those we covered in our in-depth test sites.

Overall, the conclusions were clear—people are more pro-change in their behaviors and approaches to specific changes at work as well as more pro-change in their general attitudes toward change. People are also more emotionally intelligent than previously thought. This is a rather stunning conclusion when it has been thought in some circles that emotional intelligence has been diminishing in the population. Again, our research showed the opposite with strong emotional intelligence across the board. There were a few anti-change people but those that were anti-change were that way due to poor leadership or conditions in their organization at the time of the survey. That is, when it came down to explaining why any person or group might demonstrate anti-change behavior or lower emotional intelligence, the "blame" is squarely on the specifics of the situation and/or poor leadership and management and not on people in general. Attitudes and behaviors are strongly positive overall, but can be made negative when situations suggest that being pro-change is not in one's self interest. This is completely consistent with our phase one research results.

CHAPTER 8

A New Group of Participants

At the end of the first phase of our research, we felt we had learned some interesting things about people living and working post 9/11. We perceived they were strongly pro-change, more than we might have thought and certainly more than organizational evidence seemed to suggest. We also found from our research that they were more mature and sophisticated in their thinking than might have been imagined. Finally, we realized that the ways in which people focused their attention and made decisions were more personal—that is, that family, career and health drove decisions on when and how to change. Corporate directives and efforts to externally motivate change did not appear to be the factors influencing people's decisions on change.

People were also developing in ways that were for some related to 9/11, and for others related to their own transformation efforts as a result of unique life experiences. We began to observe as well that the cultural and global forces we referred to in Part I seemed to be making an impact. For example, the desire and belief in self-help and the possibility of deep change seems to have permeated the thinking and behavior of some of our participants—especially men whose pro-change stances were at the same levels as women's, which we found counter-intuitive by surveying the media's perceptions of who is and who is not pro-change.

As consultants working in organizations, we wanted to know more. Specifically, we wanted to know about people working in organizations of various types and how they were feeling about change. We were curious if they were more or less pro-change than the random general population we had surveyed and interviewed. And we wanted to determine how situations impacted the way they handled and adapted to change. We also wanted to look closely at what was happening in various organizations to understand how the specifics of those situations were impacting the change feelings and actions of the subjects. We knew if we could capture some data that would illuminate the current state of workers in specific settings, and we could analyze how pro-change or open to change they were, we might offer some additional insights to individuals, leaders of organizational change initiatives, and organizations as a whole about how best to work with people in this early 21st century.

We wondered as well if our first phase data was too pro-change. When we went to actual work sites and did surveys with only employees, would we find the openness to change we observed when we surveyed the "public"?

We also decided to consider measuring the change reaction and emotional intelligence of change consultants themselves who were involved with change on a professional level. Collectively, the consultants we surveyed earn millions of dollars offering advice and counsel to those corporations and individuals that make change decisions and leadership choices related to transformation at work. We thought it might be interesting to consider their responses as well to determine how *they* were more or less open to change.

At this point, Dr. Thanos Patelis became more involved in the research design and thinking about how to best capture needed data and then understand and consider the feeling around change of people at work. Together we explored a number of options, including developing an original instrument as was done in phase one. What we found after much reading and reflection were two tools, already validated, that would help us get the types of insight we were looking for. Those instruments were HRDQ's Change Reaction, and Hay Associates' Emotional Intelligence Inventory. We worked with both these organizations to get permission to use their instruments. Both groups seemed as curious as we were in terms of what we might discover using their instruments.

In this chapter we will discuss both instruments as well as the other parts of research—a demographic questionnaire and a semi-structured interview of selected organizations. We will cover what they are designed to measure, how we decided to use these tools, and what we found with our new total population (phase two population 647 versus 315 for phase one). We will also discuss the new participants we sought out and present the demographics of this new 647-participant population. Finally, we will cover how the total group responded to these measures considering gender and our previously mentioned age cohorts.

Chapters 9 and 10 of this section will detail findings for the eight work sites and our organizational consultants with commentary on each situation. We will compare the total group responses to each of the site responses and the independent consultant responses to determine any differences. Since the eight sites involve a range of organizations, the reader may wish to focus on whichever organization most closely reflects one's own to determine how participants handled questions regarding change, optimism, empathy, and more, including clusters of competencies such as social awareness and relationship management. A summary of our findings in phase two of our research is found in Chapter 11 at the end of Part III. Appendix A in this chapter highlights more detailed statistical analysis information on our research with the emotional intelligence tool.

We wanted this phase of our research to have a larger sample than our first, representing a wide variety of workers at various levels within an organization and in various industries. We also wanted to attempt to get a mix of racial groups. We had somewhat of a difficult time getting the range and mix of workers we wanted. We also struggled to get a good mix of sites, interviewing and considering over 25 organizations before finally working with eight, plus our group of independent consultants (all from different consulting groups). Since some participants seem to have difficulty in identifying their industry, choosing in some cases two different industries, we are not as confident that the mix of industries described is accurate. Also, about 166 people of our total group marked "other" for industry although we provided a range of choices we thought covered most of them.

The eight sites and consultants we utilized provided roughly 250 responses for the second phase of our research. Within sites workers were recruited to answer the survey and often selected to answer it. It was not a case of randomly sending out the survey and having anyone who wanted to respond. This allows us to feel confident that the mix provided by the sites is indicative of the group within each site we were trying to sample. The remainder of the participants in phase two of our research was actively recruited to participate based on the mix of people we wanted. We worked with a company who specializes in providing participants to make certain that we would get a mix of people based on gender, age, level, and type of work as well as industry. Due to this effort, our final demographics provide a wide range of working people, representing a significant sampling of the current workforce in the United States. A small percentage of the respondents worked outside the United States, since one of our sites was based in Australia while another, a global pharmaceutical giant, has businesses globally, with participants in multiple locations.

We specifically selected key industries to look at. We thought retail, for instance, would give us access to a widely employed and growing group of workers that are not often tapped in research studies. We wanted healthcare and medical because it, again, is a growing population of workers. We thought communications and finance were also large employers, representing more complex-type business organizations. Our specific sites also sought a mix of types and styles of organizations, including: a large federal government agency and large state government agency; a 40-year old small boutique type "Wall Street" financial services firm with under 50 employees; a 15-year old international company with 2,500 employees focusing on the animal care business; a high technology company specializing in the unique aviation niche within government and industry listed as one of the top growing small firms in America; a 100-year old global pharmaceutical giant with over 150,000 employees; a small niche international design and manufacturing organization focusing on scientific applications for the blind; and a 30-year old communications firm with over 2,500 employees that provides integrated print and electronic billing and customer communications for large insurance, healthcare, utilities, and financial services companies.

The following four tables show the specific demographics of our phase two population.

Table 1 Gender Distribution of Respondents (N=647)

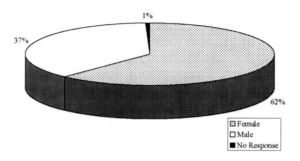

Table 2. Age Distribution of Respondents (N=647)

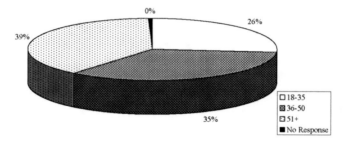

Table 3. Racial/Ethnic Distribution of Respondents (N=647)

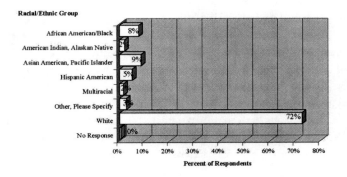

Table 4. Type of Industry Distribution of Respondents (N=856)

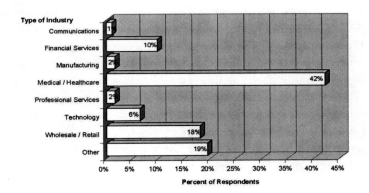

Note: The type of industry has more responses than the number of respondents, because some respondents selected more than one type. In some cases people may not have responded to a description of a person's firm as we would. For example, we worked with a manufacturing site and yet not all the workers there indicated they were in manufacturing—perhaps they considered themselves in a technology or service firm.

Our most basic questions concerned how pro-change people were in organizational life. The HRDQ Change Reaction tool is directly related to our interest. The model developed for this tool suggests that people have one of three main reactions to change at work. The first are those that are moving toward or who could be characterized as "supporting" change. An example of a statement this group would agree on would be: "I try to find out how the change might affect me," or "I am comfortable leading the change." The second are described as noncommittal and typically "moving away" from change. HRDQ calls this group "neutral" toward organizational change. Examples of statements these people might agree with are: "I don't get significantly involved," or "I take an impartial position." Finally, we have those people who in the HRDQ model would be described as "resistant to change." They might agree with statements like: "I openly resist the changes at work," or "I am not open with my dissent." The authors of the Change Reaction instrument are Drs. John Jones (recently deceased) and William Bearley—both recognized experts in the field of organizational change and development, with extensive corporate and academic credentials.

The Change Reaction (CR) tool is comprised of 24 questions answered on a five-point Likert scale (i.e., 4 is Almost Always, 3 is Very Often, 2 is Sometimes, 1 is Not Very Often, and 0 is Almost Never). Responses to these questions represented three dimensions: supportive, resistant, and neutral to change. Each dimension consisted of eight questions. The dimension scores are obtained by adding the responses to each question associated with that dimension. The internal consistency using coefficient alpha based on the sample in this study was 0.60, whereas the internal consistency for the supportive, resistant, and neutral to change dimensions was 0.70, 0.71, and 0.52, respectively. In terms of the validity evidence, this scale has been used in professional settings as a mechanism for screening individuals for their self-report on their type of response to change. No large-scale validation studies have been found.

Let's consider how the 642 people (our total population of 647) responded to the Change Reaction tool. The mean is simply the average score. The median is the score that is *literally* in the middle of the pack, and finally, the standard deviation relates to the variance among answers.

Table 5. Descriptive Statistics for CR

Area	N	Mean	Median	Std. Deviation
Supportive	644	19.0	19.0	4.43
Neutral	642	12.8	13.0	3.67
Resistant	642	6.7	6.0	3.82

The scale associated with the CR is from 0 to 4, representing the following scale: 4 is Almost Always, 3 is Very Often, 2 is Sometimes, 1 is Not Very Often, and 0 is Almost Never. There are eight questions from the CR that represent each area. The minimum is zero and the maximum score for each area is 32.

This data states that the average score for the supportive score (which could have been as high as 32 and as low as 0) was almost 19. The average for neutral was lower—about 13 out of a possible 32, and finally resistant had an average score for all participants of about 6.50 out of a possible 32. On its face, that means most people in terms of change are more supportive than they are neutral, and more neutral than they are resistant. This is overall consistent with our phase one findings.

The standard deviation is a way to determine how much variety there is within a sample of responses. The more data you have, for example the more participants who take a test, the more you will have extreme highs and lows. However, it is also true that it does not matter how large a sample, you will still have a common range of variation, even as larger samples produce more "outliers." The most common way to describe the range of variation is standard deviation. When you have data that is "normally distributed" such as that in our sample, it would follow that 68% of participants are within one standard deviation of the mean (in either direction—above or below it) and about 95% are within two standard deviations. Simply put, if our mean is 18.98 and our standard deviation 4.43, then 95% of our sample answered between 10.12 and 27.84, and 68% were between 14.55 and 23.41 (out of 32) in terms of being supportive.

Even more simply, the phase two research sample is strongly supportive of change versus neutral or resistant. We would have to note that although our total group is clearly more supportive than neutral or resistant, the mean score is not quite as high as predicted by the first phase of research. In other words, our phase two research does suggest that once in an organizational setting, the strongly pro-change attitudes found in phase one of our research are less starkly highly pro-change.

Table 6, which follows, provides a visual look at how our phase two total population responded to the Change Reaction Tool. It becomes clearer that although obviously more pro-change than neutral or resistant, the answers are not, as just noted, as starkly pro-change as our phase one data. If the scores were more starkly pro-change, the range for supportive would be closer to the 32 score.

Table 6. Summary of Scores on the Change Reaction (N= 642)

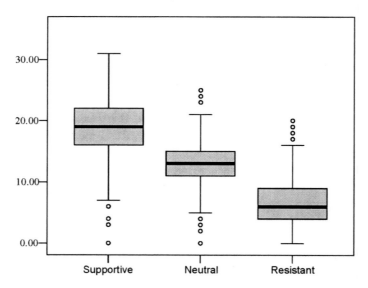

Table 6 illustrates the distribution of the scores on each dimension. The bar within each box represents the median. The median indicates where the middle of the distribution of scores falls. The top and bottom of each box represent where the middle 50% of the distribution of scores falls for each dimension. The distribution is fairly packed around the median for each dimension. The middle 50% does not cover more than 6 points on each dimension. As can be seen, however, there are a few outliers in the distribution.

As in our phase one research, we were curious if there were any differences in the way men and women looked at and handled change. As you may recall, phase one suggested few differences between the genders. Table 7 considers how our phase two group differed on the Change Reaction tool. And, as with phase one, we find little if any differences between the groups. The minor differences were that men were somewhat more supportive of change and slightly less neutral. Both groups were about the same in terms of resistance to change. The stereotype of the change resistant male is once again unsubstantiated by our research sample.

Table 7. Tiny Gender Differences are seen in Each Dimension of the Change Reaction

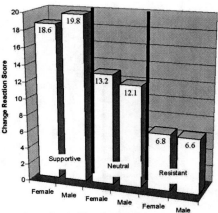

What about our age groups? Did different age groups have different change reactions? Our data mixes some of the previously discussed cohorts. However, with some minor thinking, one can make the connection. Ys (born since 1978) and Xers (born between abut 1960 and 1978/80) make up the 18-35-year old group, the Boomers (roughly born 1943-1963) make up the bulk of the 35-50-year old group, although that group does hold Xers. The 51-plus group would be mainly Boomers with some Veterans (born prior to 1943 and still working). As you may recall from our earlier discussion, research on generations at work seem to suggest that the Ys and Xers are more comfortable and supportive of change than the older Boomers and Veterans. But, as in our phase one data, this did not seem to be the case for our phase two sample.

In fact, as in phase one, the age groups had even less difference between them than did the genders. Once again, there appears to be somewhat of a myth that younger people in the workplace are more supportive of and open to change than older workers. If organizations think it would be easier to change a company with all younger people than one filled with older employees, our data would suggest that there would be little or no advantage to the younger population OR the older population. Table 8 visualizes this analysis.

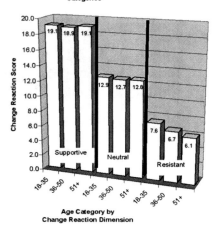

Table 8. No Differences are Seen in Each Dimension of the Change Reaction Across Age Categories

Perhaps no other concept of leadership and staff development has had wider acceptance than the concept of emotional intelligence. When Daniel Goleman wrote his first book on emotional intelligence, he likely did not realize how strongly he would touch a cord in the organizational world. *Working with Emotional Intelligence* (Goleman, 1998), has been an organizational bestseller, pointing out that the most significant type of intelligence that determines actual success or failure on the job is not the traditional intelligence measures such as mathematical and language proficiencies, but rather emotional intelligence. This constellation of skills and competencies appears to make the major difference in terms of performance at work. While traditional intelligence is generally needed to enter many work-related professions, its presence by no means predicts success. In fact, the more difficult the field of endeavor, the more complex and multidimensional emotional intelligence has more predictive abilities to determine who will succeed in businesses and organizational settings.

Common sense, or common knowledge, may suggest just the opposite. If one were to watch reality TV and see programs like *"The Apprentice,"* one might come to believe that dishonesty, insincerity, and bullying tactics win the day. But the real REALITY is that emotional intelligence matters and is well-researched in actual work settings. While the atypical CEO might get publicity, the vast majority of successful working people use high emotional intelligence to perform and excel at their jobs.

Dr. Goleman's work outlines five main areas of emotional intelligence. For each he details the sub-skills that are part of the behavior repertoire of one with this competence. Through many work examples and studies, he strongly makes the case for mastery of emotional intelligence as a means to success in any job or career—especially the ones on the way up the ladder. The more education and experience needed, the more emotional intelligence plays a significant role in the differentiation of success of any group of workers. For example, one could consider business executives at the highest levels, CEO or CFO. In studies, it is emotional intelligence that makes the difference between excellent and superior performance since most CEOs and CFOs have similar education and other work credentials.

Because anyone who aspires to high or specialized levels of work has "smarts" and education of the kind needed for entry to this job category, the importance of emotional intelligence plays a greater role in differentiating people at the top. We would strongly suggest to our readers who are unfamiliar with these concepts that they consider reading at least Goleman's basic text to gain an understanding of the critical importance and developmental issues of emotional intelligence. This is basic and required information for people working in modern organizations.

But our work is about change as we consider how best to create and support change in an ever-changing world. And we are concerned with how well people are change-positive, that is able and willing to embrace or lead change. How did we decide to use a tool designed to study emotional intelligence and use it as something related to being pro-change? Our thinking was simple. We felt that only those who perceived themselves to be highly emotionally intelligent would be likely to both reach for and develop change both within them and at work.

As change consultants, we also know that the ability to change oneself, and the ability to model the behavior wanted in others, is strongly correlated with success in changing and leading others. Many studies of excellent leaders have made the point that modeling the behaviors sought in others is one of the most highly successful change strategies. In his newest work, *Changing Minds: The Art and Science of Changing Our Own and Other People's Minds* (2004), Howard Gardner makes a strong case for this point, exploring various times when leaders succeeded or failed in changing minds. His research found that those who were not able to model what they wanted others to do tended to fail badly in making the needed changes in others.

Similarly, if people have strong social skills and can manage relationships across a range of people in a multitude of situations, they can handle and be involved with complex situations that would arise out of a change initiative. "Being pro-change" or "a change catalyst" is one of Dr. Goleman's sub-skills. We choose not to focus on just that one skill. Rather, after we studied the survey tool and worked with it through our research, we felt that it made more sense to look at the four clusters in the Emotional Competency Inventory (the model in the text has five components—all the skills are part of four clusters in the inventory). By looking at the main groups of skills, we would determine how our participants are emotionally intelligent in a broader scope, thus in our minds, more open and willing to make needed changes for success.

The four clusters are: self-awareness, self-management, social awareness, and relationship management. Self-awareness is the ability to know oneself. That self-knowledge in Goleman's model also means knowing one's strengths and weaknesses and acting self-confident in one's true and reality-based abilities. Self-management includes a solid amount of self-regulation—the managing of one's emotions when under pressure or stress. A self-regulating person does not just react to events; she or he handles them once they have thought about them. Self-management also includes being adaptive, flexible, optimistic, and open— all skills needed in our minds for dealing with change. Social awareness includes a large dose of empathy—the ability to really understand others and then to act sensitively and appropriately towards them. Organizational awareness is also part of the social awareness cluster, as is having a strong service orientation. Finally, there is the area of relationship management. This cluster includes being a change catalyst, handling conflict, developing and leading others, and having the ability to collaborate and work on a team. Again, all of these skills in one way or another help a person deal with and handle change effectively.

The Emotional Competence Inventory (ECI) is a 72-question self-report inventory measuring a person's emotional intelligence according to the work of Goleman (1998). Even though the inventory may be used to report an individual's standing on emotional intelligence by having people with various types of relationships to the individual complete the form, only the self-reported version was used for this study. The ECI as just noted above provides information on four clusters and 18 competencies. The clusters include: (1) self-awareness, (2) self-management, (3) social awareness, and (4) relationship management. The 18 competencies include: (1) accurate self-assessment, (2) emotional self-awareness, (3) self-confidence, (4) achievement orientation, (5) adaptability, (6) emotional self-control, (7) initiative, (8) optimism, (9) transparency, (10) empathy, (11) organizational awareness, (12) service orientation, (13) change catalyst, (14) conflict management, (15) developing others, (16) influence, (17) inspirational leadership, and (18) teamwork and collaboration. The overall internal consistency using coefficient alpha from the sample in this study was 0.93. The formal definition of each competency is indicated in Appendix B at the end of this chapter. The internal consistency for the clusters and competencies is shown here in Table 9.

This table helps to further clarify why we chose to look and consider clusters of skills versus individual sets of skills. Let's take just a moment to explain the term "internal consistency." The internal consistency of a score means the likelihood this same group would answer in the same way were we to conduct another test on them. Internal consistency scores that are lower than 70% do not have the consistency we want to see. Therefore, we determined that for our purposes we would look primarily at the scores of the four clusters.

Table 9. Internal Consistency of Emotional Competence Inventory (ECI) for each Cluster and Competency (Number of Items in Parentheses)

Cluster	Competency (4 for each)	Internal Consistency
Self-Awareness (12)		0.77
	Accurate Self-Assessment	0.58
	Emotional Self-Awareness	0.62
	Self-Confidence	0.66
Self-Management (24)		0.85
	Achievement Orientation	0.72
	Adaptability	0.42
	Emotional Self-Control	0.69
	Initiative	0.50
	Optimism	0.70
	Transparency	0.49
Social-Awareness (12)		0.77
	Empathy	0.60
	Organizational Awareness	0.57
	Service Orientation	0.85
Relationship Management (24)		0.90
	Change Catalyst	0.73
	Conflict Management	0.49
	Developing Others	0.71
	Influence	0.70
	Inspirational Leadership	0.73
	Teamwork & Collaboration	0.50

Below is Table 10 that shows the mean scores for each of our clusters. As just noted, the internal consistency of individual skills is not as high and hence not as accurate as those for the clusters.

Table 10. Mean Scores on each Cluster of the ECI (N=644)

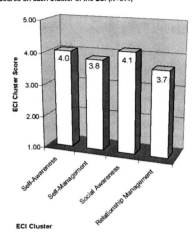

Although we did not focus on the individual skills within the clusters due to the consistency issues stated above, we did want to make the scores available to those who would be interested. They are in Appendix A of this chapter.

As Table 10 visualized, our total population is strongest in social awareness and self-awareness, and relatively less strong in self-management and relationship management. Relationship management is the weakest of all, likely due to conflict management which had the lowest of the individual skill scores. In considering whether our total sample is emotionally intelligent enough to handle change, it is clear they are quite well-equipped to handle change. Although not "perfect," our sample "sometimes" or "often" demonstrated the use of many of these skills and clusters related to emotional intelligence and hence, in our view, have the right skills to be open to and handle change in a positive manner. We were particularly pleased with the high levels of self- and social-awareness that indicates people are in touch with themselves, understand themselves, and understand others. These are vital to the process of being involved in or leading a change initiative. We do realize that by only using a self-score, we limited the effect of our research. We know that it would have been even more helpful to understand people's emotional intelligence by doing a 360 on each participant (note, a '360' is an approach that asks those reporting to someone, and those to whom one reports, to evaluate the individual in addition to their own personal self-evaluation), which was not practical or possible. But we still feel confident that these scores are meaningful. People know themselves to a large extent—not perfectly, of course, but with enough validity for us to feel confident that our total sample is quite well-equipped to handle and lead change at work. As with the change reaction tool, the emotional intelligence instrument did not suggest

90

the nearly perfect capability for change. But it is consistent with our phase one research. It is only when we went into specific sites that we began to see some differences in how people feel about and can handle change.

We were, of course, curious if our men and women and age cohorts would show differences. In phase one, our research did not show many differences between these groups, even though research previously conducted by others apparently has shown some of these differences. And, as just noted, our Change Reaction tool also did not demonstrate any differences between men and women. Table 11 that follows continues to support our research that suggests few or no differences between the sexes. Our men and women scored almost identically, with men very slightly in front of women in each cluster. One explanation of this very minor difference might be that men score themselves better than women. But in any case, the scores are so close that we saw them as virtually the same, demonstrating, as in phase one, that men and women do not seem too different in these elements in the workplace. Since our sample was made up entirely of working people, this is an important caveat.

Table 11. No Gender Differences are Seen Across Each ECI Cluster (N=400 Female and 241 Male Respondents)

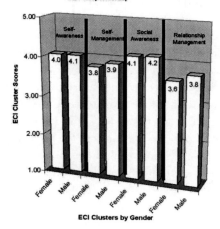

What about age? In phase one, we had originally speculated that age cohorts might deal with change differently. This did not hold true in our research, where all groups were pro-change and the most pro-change were the older groups. Nor was there any difference by age in the first part of our phase two research, using the Change Reaction tool. Was this the same for emotional intelligence? Did our younger cohorts have lower emotional intelligence scores, and therefore less ability to deal with change than our older groups? Once again, we found that there were little if any differences by age in this part of our research. This again might suggest a certain leveling force for ages when they are all working in organizations.

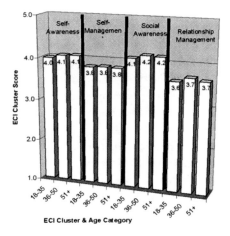

Table 12. Mean ECI Cluster Scores by Age Category (N=644)

The final part of phase two research was a semi-structured questionnaire that we used to get a "picture" of the organizations where we did research. The questions we asked were related to current changes the organization was going through, or those they had just gone through. We developed a profile of each site which gives an idea of the organization, its work, and its current change climate. Then, for the purposes of determining if there were differences in the responses based on the culture, leadership, and situation—as we perceived it and as the scores of the total group indicated—we would share that as well.

We decided to group the eight sites in the following way. First, we selected those organizational sites where we felt the culture and leadership were most pro-change and provided a setting where people could properly respond to change and participate in it effectively. Four sites fell into this category. The second group we described as being a mixed bag, with some good things happening, but many questions about how the organization as a whole seemed to be dealing with change and how the leadership was providing appropriate leadership in the change situations presented to their people at the time the site was surveyed. In some cases, we were able to go back and get an update and some additional data, which helped us understand the situations more fully. Four organizations were placed in the "mixed bag" category due to our concerns about culture, leadership, or both. We put the consultants in the more positive group, believing that their impact on the organizations they were working with would be a positive one.

What we then considered, which is detailed in the next two chapters, is how people responded against the total population in both the more positive pro-change settings, and the less effective "mixed bag" change settings. We neither saw differences in gender nor ages, and we began wondering if we would see some differences in how people responded to these tools.

We asked our contacts at the sites to select a sample of workers at different professional levels, genders, ages, and races to get a random sample of the workers in the part of the organization we were studying. This approach provided us with a mix of people and no bias in terms of self-selection.

As noted, in Chapters 9 and 10 we discuss the eight sites and our independent consultants. For each we provide situational information based on our interviews, and then provide statistics comparing how they responded to both the change instrument and the emotional intelligence inventory versus our total population, which included them as well as all other sites and participants. We end each site discussion with some short commentary on how and why this site group may have answered as they did, finally drawing some conclusions. Chapter 11 provides a summary of the results of phase two of our research.

Appendix A

Descriptive Statistics for each cluster and each sub skill in the ECI

Cluster	Competency	N	Mean	Std. Deviation
Self-Awareness		644	4.05	0.51
	Accurate Self Assessment	644	3.97	0.53
	Emotional Self Awareness	644	3.98	0.61
	Self Confidence	469	4.09	0.58
Self-Management		644	3.84	0.47
	Achievement Orientation	644	3.84	0.65
	Adaptability	641	3.96	0.62
	Emotional Self-Control	642	3.77	0.64
	Initiative	643	3.56	0.76
	Optimism	644	4.09	0.65
	Transparency	644	3.86	0.73
Social Awareness		644	4.14	0.55
	Empathy	644	4.26	0.53
	Organizational Awareness	469	3.69	0.71
	Service Orientation	644	4.32	0.83
Relationship Management		644	3.67	0.55
	Change Catalyst	643	3.55	0.71
	Conflict Management	644	2.99	0.76
	Developing Others	644	3.98	0.70
	Influence	469	3.60	0.79
	Inspirational Leadership	644	3.76	0.77
	Teamwork and Collaboration	644	4.12	0.60

Because of a technical malfunction, some of the questions of the ECI for some of the respondents were not presented and some data were lost. Therefore, some competencies have fewer respondents than others. Each competency is reported from a scale of 1 to 5, with 1 representing never, 2 representing rarely, 3 representing sometimes, 4 representing often, and 5 representing consistently.

Appendix B
Definitions of Emotional Competence Inventory (ECI) Competencies

Competency	Definition
Accurate Self-Assessment	Knowing one's inner resources, abilities, and limits.
Achievement Orientation	Striving to improve or meeting a standard of excellence.
Adaptability	Flexibility in handling change.
Change Catalyst	Initiating or managing change.
Conflict Management	Negotiating and resolving disagreements.
Developing Others	Sensing others' development needs and bolstering their abilities.
Emotional Self-Awareness	Recognizing how our emotions affect our performance.
Emotional Self-Control	Keeping disruptive emotions and impulses in check.
Empathy	Sensing others' feelings and perspectives, and taking an active interest in their concerns.
Influence	Having impact on others.
Initiative	Readiness to act on opportunities.
Inspirational Leadership	Inspiring and guiding individuals and groups.
Optimism	Persistence in pursuing goals despite obstacles and setbacks
Organizational Awareness	Reading a group's emotional currents and power relationships.
Self-Confidence	A strong sense of one's self-worth and capabilities.
Service Orientation	Anticipating, recognizing, and meeting customers' or clients' needs.
Teamwork and Collaboration	Working with others towards a shared goal. Creating group synergy in pursuing collective goals.
Transparency	Maintaining integrity, acting congruently with one's values.

CHAPTER 9

Sites that Shined

In the next two chapters we detail the eight sites and the independent consultant group we surveyed. In analyzing the eight sites, we considered information about them gathered through staff interviews, their web site, and other public domain information. The interviews we had with people at the organization gave us some background on the organization, its recent history with change, and its culture and leadership style. Organizations are disguised by changing names, locations, and certain nonconsequential details. However, site descriptions of these organizations provide an accurate picture of their relative size, operations, culture, leadership, and recent issues with change in the part of the organization we studied.

After studying our eight sites, we selected four of them that we felt were more "pro-change" oriented. Our criteria for this was that the culture, leadership strategies, and general conditions at the time of the survey were likely, in our professional judgment, to allow staff to contribute and feel part of the change process in a positive way. It was our guess that these participants would score higher on their openness to change and emotional intelligence.

For each of the less "pro-change" sites described in Chapters 9 and 10, we provide some background on the specific site and/or group, figures that compare how the site participants answered the two major tools we used—the change reaction tool and the emotional intelligence inventory. In each case, we compare the answers of the given site with the total group that responded to these surveys. Following these figures, we provide a brief commentary on the interrelationship between their answers and the specifics of the site.

It is our hope that these specific sites provide some additional insight into how the culture and industry a given group is in may impact their responses to the surveys or to any intervention planned. In this way, change agents, leaders, and individuals can make an assessment of their own actions and consider the logical anticipated outcome.

This chapter focuses on our four pro-change sites: Worldwide Wellness, a 100,000 plus employee global healthcare giant; Integrated Communications, Inc. a 50 year old, 1500 person, communications company providing integrated call center services and cutomer communication solutions to many of the country's largest insurance, healthcare, utilities and financial services companies; Northeast State Court Operations, a large court system of a major eastern state; and finally, Global Life Sciences, a 15-year old, 2,600 person animal care business providing a range of products to veterinarians. Each has an interesting history and is faced with different challenges and opportunities. We hope you will find their stories of interest.

Worldwide Wellness

Worldwide Wellness is over 100 years old and operates in over 57 countries, serving in excess of 175 different companies and employing over 100,000 people. It is a recognized leader in helping to heal, cure, and provide quality of life to those with health related issues. Their history is one of constant growth and a foundation built on a shared sense of values and core beliefs based on a credo developed early in the organization's history. As a recognized leader and provider of quality products, Worldwide Wellness prides itself on change and the ability to handle it with passion and focus. Employees are expected to lead and participate in change all the time. The company believes in customer focus and making certain that products and services are always being researched and developed to meet the ever-changing needs of its worldwide customer base.

The organization went through some major change in the last few years as its long-time President passed the baton to another chief executive. In many ways, there were few real changes since the current President was an insider who, like his predecessors, took control of an organization with long-held processes and standard, professional approaches to change and leadership. Although some new acquisitions and organizational changes were made, these were not unexpected or unusual in how they were managed and introduced to the organizational culture.

The company has, in fact, made a commitment to staff development that includes an emphasis on helping people be pro-change and handle it effectively. They had championed research by leading experts on how best to train and develop people to be leaders of change and collaborate with people across boundaries. That said, the realities of business and its fast pace does not always allow for all the people all the time to handle change appropriately and to act with strong emotional intelligence.

We chose to do our research with a group within this global giant that was focused on educating young and new workers in the organization. As part of the Technical Leadership Development Process, there is a tough screening process for technical professionals to help select those people who the organization believes have the best chance of developing into global leaders, are experts in both technology and leadership, and can help the organization maintain its edge in markets around the world. For the last five years, the organization has selected about 40 or 50 staff members to participate in this rotational development program with the idea that these young people can become leaders in the next decades. All who enter the program have recently completed their undergraduate or graduate studies and appear to have the right mix of technical and professional skills as well as an openness to learning and growth.

While the selection process is tight and theoretically attracts very highly desirable candidates, the reality is the group is still young. The experts leading the program have determined that emotional intelligence (EI) is the key factor that will determine how well these individuals will fare as time moves on. Due to this, development programs focusing on EI issues are provided to all those in the program early in the developmental cycle, ensuring that they are both aware of and focused on strengthening these skills.

The designers of the Technical Leadership Development Process thought that determining how well or not some of its participants were faring in EI and change in general would be a unique opportunity to determine how their efforts to focus attention on EI were working.

Although not a perfect organization by any means, Worldwide Wellness has the culture, processes, and leadership in place for needed change—especially in the area we were surveying that supports and encourages involvement, proper enthusiasm for needed change, and a pro-active approach to handling and dealing effectively with change situations. We felt pretty confident they would do well on both tools.

Table 13. Mean Scores on the Change Reaction Scale for Worldwide Wellness (n=36) Compared to All Respondents (n=642)

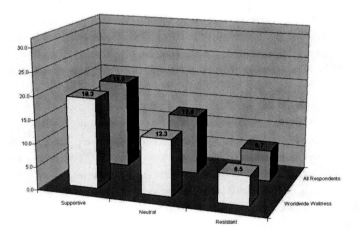

Table 14 Mean Scores on the Emotional Competence Inventory for Worldwide Wellness (n=36)

Compared to All Respondents (n=642)

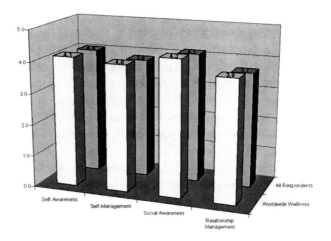

Commentary:

As predicted, Worldwide Wellness did extraordinarily well on both instruments. The scores of respondents from Worldwide Wellness on both the Change Reaction (CR) and the Emotional Competency Inventory (ECI) were similar to the scores of all respondents. Where there were minor differences, the Worldwide Wellness people did better than our overall participant group. Even in the challenging area of relationship management, this group did better than our overall group, suggesting that they have training or at least exposure to processes and approaches that help them deal effectively with conflict. The data suggests that the program (a specific leadership focused effort) these people were in and the overall company culture contributed to these strong scores. Our thinking is that they would be even stronger if the group were older and more seasoned.

Integrated Communications, Inc.

Integrated Communications, Inc. (ICI) is a communications company founded more than 50 years ago. It focuses on providing integrated call center services and customer communication solutions to many of the country's largest insurance, healthcare, utilities, and financial services companies. Every month ICI handles hundreds of thousands of calls and delivers bills, statements, explanations of benefits, and other business critical customer communications. The company has over 1,500 employees and revenues of over $250 million in 2003. There are multiple call centers and production facilities within the United States and internationally.

The expertise of the company is quite high. ICI provides services to five of the top ten wireless providers; four of the top multiple systems operations; eight of the top ten fund complexes; four of the top ten brokerage firms; and four of the top ten defined contribution providers. ICI has extensive expertise in the utilities, healthcare, and insurance industries, as well as serving many of the top providers in these businesses. Simply put, ICI is an inbound and outbound communications powerhouse.

The company web site is filled with multiple references from companies in each of their defined markets. Here are a few samples. "By outsourcing our billing function to ICI, we got a competitive jump on the launch of our new financial services product." Or, "We chose ICI because they had the best solution and the most experience." Or," With the support of ICI, we can provide value-added services to our customers to help them provide superior service to their own clients." .

ICI has alliances with three types of organizations. The first are customer call management systems and billing services solution partners. The second type of alliance includes solutions and technology partners. Finally, ICI has marketing partners, including a leading processor of consumer to business electronic payments.

ICI, like many organizations, has gone through major changes and reorganizations over the last number of years. The company underwent significant consolidation and reorganization four years ago to ensure greater customer satisfaction and improved profitability. Throughout all of this change, ICI has remained a viable player in a smaller market with a limited number of competitors. Like many businesses, the services offered by ICI are "a commodity," making it especially important that the company continue to add value while meeting and exceeding customer expectations.

The executive we spoke with saw himself as a change agent. He saw his role as driving change throughout the organization, making it more aware of the continuous need for improvements, and making every customer a reference. Part of this executive's focus was dismantling silos between groups such as client services and systems so that there would be a stronger and more aligned focus on the customer. The executive we spoke with stressed the importance of changing the culture to be more team-oriented and seamless between areas. This idea of focusing on teams is a common theme in modern business where the ability of a company to have its staff work together becomes increasingly important to create improved quality and service.

The leadership of ICI has changed as well. Formerly a traditional company tied to its Midwest roots, the new management team seems more willing to take risks and move into more innovative technologies. Consolidation of facilities has taken place and layoffs have occurred. The consolidation has actually increased production capacity. On the people side, the usual upset of facility consolidations and layoffs has receded some as those who remain or are new accept and understand that the layoffs were necessary to keep the business profitable.

The new management has done a good job of communicating with the remaining staff and emphasizing the renewed focus on customer care and profitability. However, as in most organizations, it is the day-to-day management, like the executive with whom we spoke, that is bearing the burden of helping people realize a new culture, cope with ongoing change, and continue to perform at ever-higher levels of productivity.

ICI appears to be continuing its journey to becoming a major player in its niche market. It is accomplishing this by navigating the waters of alliances of all types that make sense for the business while simultaneously working internally on creating a more nimble, team-based culture. Such a culture breaks down silos and old outdated caste systems and brings teams together to continue to create error-free and appropriate inbound and outbound customer communications products and services.

Table 15. Mean Scores on the Change Reaction Scale for Integrated Communications (n=36)

Compared to All Respondents (n=642)

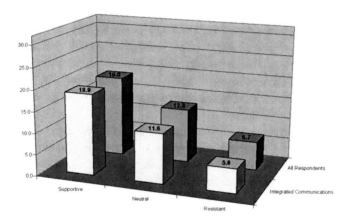

Table 16. Mean Scores on the Emotional Competence Inventory for Integrated Communications
(n=36) Compared to All Respondents (n=642)

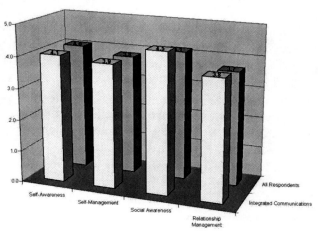

Commentary:

We had predicted that ICI would do well and they did. They were a good deal less resistant to change than our total group, and also less neutral as well as more positive toward change although by a very small measure.

As for EI, ICI was a bit more socially aware as well as skilled in relationship management. We found that the efforts of the leadership of this organization helped create these positive differences by their active intervention in the situations confronting the company. Further, we discovered that the culture of the company and its efforts in the change arena kept the scores high despite some difficult times and challenges. It is also helpful that the company is doing well and seems very committed to top level service—success breeds success and this company's pro-change policies allowed staff to feel part of a winning organization with which they were proud and actively engaged.

Northeast State Court Operations

The Northeast State Court System has a simple and clear focus: "Our mission is to promote the rule of law, and to serve the public by providing just and timely resolution of all matters before the courts. The court system is complex and ever-evolving as it seeks to work with the legislature of the state to improve the delivery of court services to people all over the state." Our research took place in the broad area of Administrative Support. Administrative Support was reorganized about five years ago as a result of a need to provide structure and organization to a system that had expanded, but was not as coordinated and effective as it might be. The courts and departments had grown, but the support organization itself was not unified and systematized. A division structure was put into place and Directors were appointed to handle specific aspects of the overall division of administrative services such as HR, Court Operations, Legal, and Technology.

The Court Operations group has grown in the last few years as it has demonstrated its efficiency and ability to carry out support all over the state. The executive in charge of Court Operations discussed her organization freely and indicated her own philosophy of leading with strong direction, strong support, and frequent praise for work well done. Her high standards and expectations of excellence, coupled with her positive leadership style, have led to a unit where more work is actually welcomed as a challenge and a recognition that past work has been well accomplished.

State governments, as with all governments, have increasingly met with resistance from taxpayers. People are aware of the need to manage responsibly and continually, and, as in the profit sector, try to "do more with less." This has led to a sense among some of the workforce, according to our executive, that that they will not be able to do what they want and need to get by with diminishing resources. This is a constant leadership challenge for the director since she is convinced that her area of Court Operations will experience ongoing expansion and growth as she and her group's efforts continue to demonstrate excellence.

An interesting aspect of the work of Court Operations is its depth and diversity as well as its approach to supporting courts locally all over the state. This particular group manages a variety of programs statewide including, but not limited to, alternative dispute resolution programs, the Americans with Disability Act as it applies in the courts, records management, legal information, and court interpreting services developed as a result of a lawsuit against the state.

The Division of Court Operations operates almost like a consulting firm. They see each county where courts exist as a client with unique and special needs and a culture that needs to be preserved. They apply themselves to making certain that the courts in each location can utilize the appropriate resources and learning opportunities that they need to properly implement programs and policies required statewide. Whether helping provide legal information, support for interpreting services, or offering guidance on how best to use alternatives to the litigation, the Division of Court Operations listens and suggests needed resources through competence, cooperation, and developed relationships and alliances across the state. With a myriad of needs and a core staff of only about 80 people, this Division is working constantly to handle the responsibilities of supporting courts throughout the state.

Change is a core part of the job of the professionals within Court Operations. They function almost as change agents for the court system. It is often the Division of Court Operations staff that is communicating about new policies on a topic like diversity and discrimination, or helping a county or court adapt to a new technology solution. They are in the forefront of encouraging productive ways that work within the rules of the legislature, but manage to streamline operations at the same time. An example would be supporting the grouping of cases involving the same people to allow for greater coordination between cases.

The executive we spoke to had much praise for the very innovative and influential chief of the courts. This judge has a widely-held superlative reputation for innovation and creativity that is helping Northeast State Court Operations work in new and innovative ways. It appears that between leadership in the state that supports change and innovation, and leadership of the area that supports the work of people to move beyond the boundaries of their job when possible (and within civil service guidelines), this organization has the culture to ensure that change and transformation is a reality.

Since 1980 or so when job cuts were real, there has not really been much destabilizing of the State Courts despite changing administrations and issues within the state itself. The people of the Court Operations division see themselves as service-oriented and focused on others. This orientation should help them continue to develop ever higher levels of competency and change resilience while continuing to implement creative solutions to statewide court challenges.

Table 17. Mean Scores on the Change Reaction Scale for Court Operations (n=23) Compared to

All Respondents (n=642)

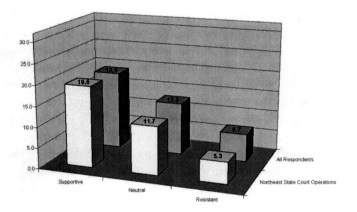

Table 18. Mean Scores on the Emotional Competence Inventory for Court Operations (n=23)

Compared to All Respondents (n=642)

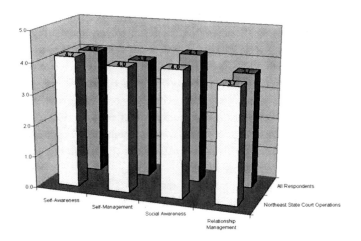

Commentary:

The strong positive scores at the Northeast Court System were generated in large part due to the exceptional positive leadership demonstrated by the executive in charge. Her savvy and sophistication allowed a group who is under-appreciated, dealing with ever-decreasing resources and ever-increasing workloads, to handle change well and be highly emotionally intelligent in the process.

While working in a politically charged and challenging environment, our leader in this situation involved and engaged the entire team in a way that made them proud to do more work, proud of their accomplishments, and able to handle complex situations easily. We do not believe that the overall culture that this group faces daily would have sustained the high scores without her strong leadership. And the existence of her strong leadership helped her group demonstrate not just a high interest in change, but lower than average adverse reactions toward change along with strong skills across the board in EI. While dealing with tight budgets, this culture allowed for scores as high as a powerful global business with all the resources in the business world. This is no small accomplishment. The idea that government types are anti-change and not forward thinking was not supported by this research; rather, this research demonstrated strength across the board despite shifts in policies, challenging state situations, and narrowing resources.

Global Life Sciences

Global Life Sciences (GLS) is a 15-year old international company headquartered in the Midwest. It focuses primarily on the animal care business providing a range of products and services to animal veterinarians. Offerings include in-clinic diagnostic tests, pharmaceuticals, and practice management software. GLS also has other lines of business that utilize their expertise in diagnostic technology. These include screening for water safety and for the health of animals like swine and cattle.

Until relatively recently, GLS's CEO was its founder. In 2002, a new CEO was brought into the company to grow the business and build on the reputation for quality and innovation that have always been part of GLS's reputation. The new CEO came from GE where he had years of experience with implementation strategies for growth and processes in every aspect of several of their businesses, including jet engines and financial services. The company has moved from being a relatively small player in the market to a major competitor. The company's goals include being twice as large as any of its closest competitors. Acquisitions have been a large part of the changes made as well. European operations have grown the most substantially as well as there being some growth in Asia. The company currently has 2,600 employees, up from 1,800 in 1998.

The company was always focused on quality and innovation. But the new CEO and the expanded leadership team he has assembled remain focused on bringing in higher skilled and more process orientated staff. While the company in its infancy thrived on an entrepreneurial culture with relatively few rules and little bureaucracy, the newer organization needs more structure if it is to continue to grow, attract top scientists, and handle the issues of the day including Sarbanes-Oxley and other increased government regulations.

The new CEO brought in more women executives and placed a premium on moving the organization from its adolescence to its early adulthood. Processes were put into place, more of a business orientation was expected from all staff, and new skill sets and competencies were established to make certain that the skills needed for the 21st century were part of the credentials for all new hires.

As GLS with its clear mission, vision, and values began to move ahead in the direction of consistent processes and needed attention to detail and structure, some were left behind. While many of the old-time staff embraced the changes, some did not. Some people felt the direction of the firm was too much of a shift in the company with which they had grown up. Some left the firm on their own while others were let go in downsizing that coincided with changes in the skill sets needed and new and increasing demands on the organization. GLS sees itself as a learning organization. There is increased emphasis on sharing resources within the organization, across lines of business, and between and among different locations. Executives from Europe and Asia are brought to the Midwest headquarters to learn and then encouraged to go back and put concepts like ISO 9000 or Six Sigma into practice. The learning is encouraged in all directions, with folks from the United States offices learning and understanding processes from Europe and Asia that might well make sense here.

GLS is in a growth market, has a stock on the rise, and is set to be at over 600 million in sales by the end of 2005. The stock range in 2004 was $38.00 to $55.00. It is expected to continue to grow as the company makes progress in keeping the competition at bay and making new discoveries that serve its customer niche markets.

GLS seems to be on solid ground financially and organizationally as it proceeds to meet its new goals and objectives for 2005. Its culture is continuing to evolve to be more flexible and yet more structured at the same time. It is relying on its new leadership team and increasingly aligned staff to support its mission and vision. While there are some lingering anxieties of longer term employees, the changes have consistently been communicated and shared in ways that are allowing more and more of the staff to get on board with needed transformation initiatives and innovations. If there was any concern with GLS, it was its tough standards and high demands that appear to be placed on all employees. Their strong growth and positive situation has been built on the hard work of hundreds of people who in some situations appear stressed despite the positive performance they are exhibiting.

Table 19. Mean Scores on the Change Reaction Scale for Global Life Sciences (n=37) Compared to All Respondents (n=642)

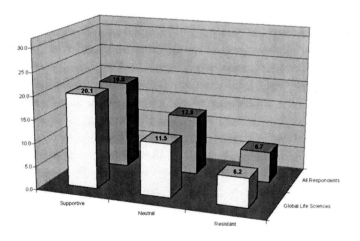

Table 20. Mean Scores on the Emotional Competence Inventory for Global Life Sciences (n=37)

Compared to All Respondents (n=642)

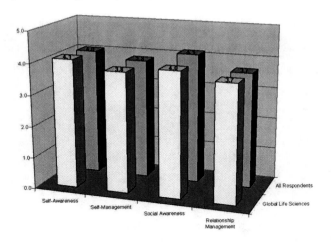

Commentary:

GLS did well. They were at the norms and close to our total group. They were highly pro-change which seems to be part of their culture, but they do retain some people who are resistant which might be due to the push-push environment we noted in the description.

GLS appears to have people who are exhibiting high EI and handling the changes with some ease; this is likely due to the fact that the organization got rid of people who were not "with the program" or who appeared unable to handle the bold direction the company set for itself. We see the scores as indicative that the efforts to get people to come on board with a strong new strategy have essentially succeeded. The company has created a can-do culture that shows up in the strong scores of its participants. Whether these will hold if too much pressure continues is an unknown, but for now, the company appears to have hit the right balance between a growth strategy and approaches to people that support involvement and commitment to change.

Independent Consultants

We asked 15 colleagues in our industry who we did not work with directly, but who worked with various companies on issues of change and growth, to participate in our research. We assumed these would be the most pro-change people we would survey. That turned out to be the case, as the figures below explain. There was one very interesting point—this group had the biggest group of resisters to change as well as the highest scores of those pro-change. We can only guess why, but we surmise that those who have led numerous change initia-

PAT GILL WEBBER

tives might be cautious about some strategies for change that assume too much
progress and too little work to make them happen. Their resistance then is based
on realism about what is possible and probable in these challenging, transformational times.

Table 21. Mean Scores on the Change Reaction Scale for Independent Consultants (n=15)

Compared to All Respondents (n=642)

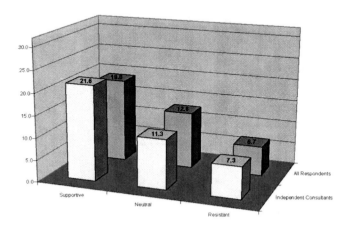

Table 22. Mean Scores on the Emotional Competence Inventory for Independent Consultants

(n=16) Compared to All Respondents (n=642)

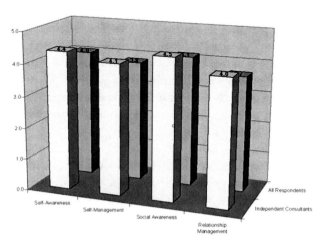

Commentary:

Since research on change suggests that "walking the talk" is the strongest way to manage change, our consultants fit the bill. They are highly pro-change, with strong emotional intelligence, and in all cases did better than the overall group in every aspect of the emotional intelligence competencies. Since in many cases they are teaching issues of emotional intelligence, this is gratifying.

CHAPTER 10

Our "Mixed Bag" Sites

In Chapter 9 we discussed the four sites where we felt the culture and leadership of the organization was setting a more pro-change and positive approach to transformation. We predicted that these sites and their participants would do better on both tools. This was true, but with very small margins. In fact, in some cases the scores were virtually identical to the larger population.

In this chapter, we look at those sites we had more concerns about. None were terrible or disastrous organizations, but we did see danger signs in these sites. We observed leadership situations which were being handled in a way that would "de-motivate" the employees, or where the leaders were not providing the right type of direction. In some cases, we saw situations where the industry or the immediate situation was so disorienting that it would be tough for any workers to feel totally open and responsive to change. We did not know if, in fact, these sites would do better or worse than the others; the chapter to follow shares with you where we were right and where we might have been less than accurate about what might occur.

In each case we discuss the site and show the results of how they responded to both the change reaction tool and the EI clusters compared to our total group. Then we share our commentary of why they may have answered as they did and our analysis of the situation.

The sites here are: Aviation Technologies, a 400-person technology firm founded in the 1980s with a backlog of work and a history of increased revenues and profits serving the government and aviation marketplaces; Visual Support Technologies, a small manufacturer of unique service products for the visually-impaired headquartered in Australia that has gone through a change in leadership; Patrick Williams and Associates, an established "Wall Street" firm that has undergone several changes in ownership in the last several years; and Special Needs Administration, a large federal government agency living with the inevitable pressures of doing more with less while serving an ever-increasing "customer" base. These were challenged sites with pressures and problems generated by their successes and the nature of changing conditions in their industries.

We end Part III with Chapter 11 which provides a summary of phase two of our research which we hope sets the stage for Chapter 12 where we provide our advice for individuals, company leaders, and organizations themselves as they work to meet the needs of the 21st century.

Aviation Technologies, Inc.

Aviation Technologies, Inc. (ATI) is a technology company founded in the late 80s by an international business executive and technology expert focused on the aviation market and supplying technology driven products and services to the government and industry. According to its web site, ATI has experienced continuous revenue growth and profitability since its inception. It currently has a contract backlog of over three years.

The company is still privately held. Its owner/founder is well respected in industry and government circles, being recognized in a number of ways by his colleagues and peers in technology and government. The executive and management team is made up of skilled engineers and computer scientists.

There are currently about 400 professionals in the company in various strategic business areas, including Tactical Systems, Information Assurance, Information Technology, Training Systems, Engineering Support, Safety Technologies, and Security Technologies. Clients include government agencies and other country governments such as the Department of Commerce and the Republic of China.

The Inc. 500 has named Aviation Technologies one of the top ten fastest-growing privately held companies. Locations include facilities on the East Coast of the United States, in Texas, and in Asia. Although originally focused solely on the aviation industry, the company continues to try to diversify its business solutions and client base. In its markets, it appears to be one of only a few companies in their niche markets. This has been a clear factor in their success in obtaining and keeping business relationships.

An executive in the division where the data was collected described the company as struggling to move from its small firm status to operating and gaining contracts as a bigger company with more formal processes and policies. This executive felt a real weakness of the organization was its territorial nature that isolated people from one division to another. He felt that there was insufficient leveraging of the internal resources the company had with various groups doing their own thing when they could have used the help of others within the organization.

It is unclear whether the diversified culture and insular approach is one that is strategically sought or just a result of the way the company is organized, with different businesses focused on targeted clients, and efforts with little overlap with other divisions.

The executive we interviewed described the relationship of his division's key client and his team as terrific and one that was close and supported by management to be a real partnership. But change was brewing due to a push to get more diverse clients, and to reach beyond the very comfortable client relationship with the key account and get more clients into the division. It is unclear how much people can, in fact, help create this goal of broader business, but it seems senior management is very interested in staff at every level being aware of their responsibility to bring in new and expanded business.

Although the company as a whole is doing well as it is described on the company web site, the division where our data was collected did have layoffs in 2004, although some folks were being rehired. At the current time, work seems to be very busy and a backlog persists due to a current contract with a large government agency.

That said, there did not appear to be anxiety over the company being sold, losing market share, or of more layoffs and downsizing. In our mind, however, layoffs nearly always create a red flag for us since downsizing of any type inevitably affects people's security and generates anxiety unless deftly handled by leadership. People know the organization has to change to meet the marketplace needs and that more diverse business is a priority, but according to our contact, they do not appear to be that anxious as a result. As noted, we wonder about that.

The last major company-wide change was three years ago when the organization was re-organized and a new COO's position was formalized from within. The COO has attempted to put more structure into the organization. This appears to be in response to some of the issues raised by the executive we spoke with and others who feel the organization needs more attention paid to developing shared and well-understood policies and procedures.

For the first time, company-wide strategic plans are being formulated and shared at Aviation Technologies, Inc. This new approach is providing all employees with a clearer idea of where the company is headed and what their contribution is to making that growth and change happen.

Since the company is privately held, and no effort is underway to change that, the executive we talked with said he felt there was a limit to the involvement and commitment employees would have since there was no way that any of them might participate in actual ownership of the enterprise. We saw this as another red flag. He also noted that although the web site described the company as employee-development focused with a priority on staff development, the overall feeling within the ranks of the company is that the organization is not primarily employee focused with strong and meaningful HR policies and procedures. Again, this is a red flag for us in terms of people's openness to change.

ATI appears to be a dynamic and exciting technology company that is sharply focused on creating excellent technology and delivering value for their clients. They do not appear to be as internally organized as they might like to be, nor do they appear to have a strong emphasis on cultural development and employee relationship and collaboration. That said, its growth and close client relationships would appear to make it a rather stable environment in an overall unstable economy.

Table 23. Mean Scores on the Change Reaction Scale for Aviation Technologies (n=15)

Compared to All Respondents (n=642)

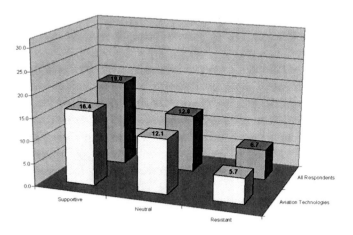

Table 24. Mean Scores on the Emotional Competence Inventory for Aviation Technologies

(n=15) Compared to All Respondents (n=642)

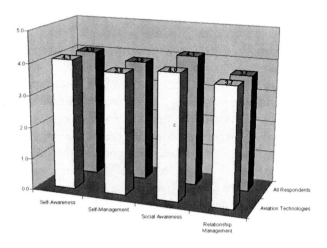

Commentary:

As predicted, ATI did poorly, relatively speaking, compared to the total

114

population. They were more resistant, and had more neutrals as well as less positive reactions to change. Given what was going on, we were surprised the scores were as good as they were.

In terms of EI, the participants surprised us by being at the norms in all four clusters. Rather than reacting negatively to the changes around them, they were still handling themselves and others in a manner that was positive. We did note that the company was attempting to involve and engage people in their new strategies. This appears to have been successful in keeping scores as high as the norm. And, as our contact had assured us, despite layoffs, the management of the situation was not causing major anxiety among the troops—or at least in any way that was lowering their EI. When we looked closer within the clusters, we did see some lower scores, but overall, despite our concerns, ATI staff held their own.

Visual Support Technologies, Inc.

Visual Support Technologies (VST) is a privately held company with worldwide offices founded in the late 1980s. Originally a one-product firm, it has evolved to sell a variety of products designed specifically for the visually impaired. The company's main office is on the west coast of the United States but there are offices in Canada, Sweden, the Netherlands, and Australia, with distribution channels throughout Europe and the Middle East.

VST is recognized around the world as a leader in the blindness and low vision industries. It provides the best customer service possible, finding fast and effective solutions for their market. Products include integrated speech and Braille technology, a range of video magnifier solutions, screen reading software, and speech synthesizes. Private agencies, eye-care professionals, schools and rehabilitation organizations, as well as home users, governments, and private agencies purchase these products. The company prides itself on a culture of dedication and the belief that everyone deserves the same opportunities.

In the last year, a new CEO has been brought in to help grow the business, increase profits, and expand the reach of the business into all available markets. He has also been charged with increasing the professionalism of the staff and developing a stronger culture of high performance and accountability. While VST has always been dedicated to its customers, its style and approach was more relaxed and less "business like" and "driven" than necessary given the global marketplace. The new CEO was specifically charged with creating a turnaround in the organization.

As part of the new CEO's vision, there will be increased personal accountability at all levels, a renewed and increased focus on product quality, and a more aggressive marketing effort to reach out to the blind and low vision community to make certain that all efforts are being made to connect to and fully represent the interests of this population. The ultimate aim is to be seen as the consistent vendor of choice within the blind and low vision community.

The CEO has made some staff changes, both letting some people go and adding others with different credentials and commitment. His vision includes providing increased opportunities for staff, and with the help of his direct reports, create systems and processes that will support the new high performance culture he is trying to achieve. While some have felt the pressure and moved on, overall there appears to be acceptance and enthusiasm for a more focused, opportunistic, high performance, and fully engaged organization. We were concerned that the new CEO might have been too strong and too direct for the culture of the company, which in many ways is laid back and "Australian" since the founder is from that part of the world. We also had issues and concerns about the owner's ability to "let go" and allow the new CEO to make the needed changes that he felt were necessary to increase company profitability.

At the time the survey was conducted, the CEO was establishing his authority and energizing the organization, but we wondered if, as noted, he might be moving too fast for some. We heard that post our survey, the original owner was upset by the CEO's insistence on new quality initiatives that would delay product launches, and would again mean a change in the culture and style of the company. We heard through our contact that the CEO had decided to leave the firm since his desires for change and new marketing and sales strategies were in too much conflict with the owner. It is unfortunate that the new CEO did leave in our view. Although we had concerns about scores in light of rapid change, the people of VST actually did better than we thought and likely could have handled the changes that were being implemented. It appears that the resistance to change was limited to the owner himself, who likely saw the organization slipping away from his direct control and resisted that movement.

Table 25. Mean Scores on the Change Reaction Scale for Visual Support Technologies (n=33) Compared to All Respondents (n=642)

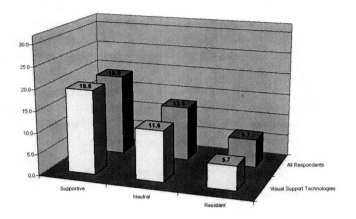

Table 26. Mean Scores on the Emotional Competence Inventory for Visual Support Technologies (n=33) Compared to All Respondents (n=642)

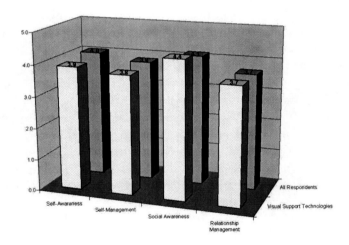

Commentary:

It appears our new CEO at VST was doing the job. The very high scores on the change reaction tool indicate that although changes were rapid and extensive, the team was very much in favor of the changes with high positives and very low

117

resistance. This would be excellent news for any new leader attempting to create large-scale change, as was the new CEO.

The scores on EI were also very high especially in social awareness. The CEO himself was one of the most highly emotionally intelligent executives we have met in many years. His strong personal skills obviously impacted his staff, who responded very positively and strongly across the board. Any reservations we had thinking that rapid changes would stop people's pro-change attitudes were proven wrong with these scores.

It is ironic that the CEO left due to the owner's desire to remain or go back to older ways of doing things. Likely had the owner reflected on how well the CEO's changes were being accepted by the entire team, he might have reconsidered the differences and concerns he had about moving ahead.

Patrick Williams and Associates

Founded over forty years ago, Patrick Williams and Associates is a full service money management firm catering to wealthy individual investors as well as to unions and other public groups who have money management needs. This company uses individual investment managers to make choices for each client on an individual basis. Fees are generated by a small percentage rate on assets of the individual or group of investors. There is an investment committee, but individual managers are free to make their own decisions on the proper allocation of stocks, bonds, and cash in any given client portfolio. The company is relatively small—about 50 employees including all managers, their assistants, back office operations people, and other support personnel. Offices are in Manhattan, Phoenix, and Connecticut.

Founded by Patrick Williams, an early value investor (similar to Warren Buffet), the company has gone through a series of changes in ownership and organization since the founder passed away about eight years ago. When the owner was in his late 80s, he sold the firm to an investor after his own son, to whom he hoped to pass on the firm, unexpectedly passed away. When the firm was first sold in 1993, Mr. Williams continued to come into work each day until his death at 100. A few remaining members of the Williams family continued to work with the firm as money managers until the final year when the last granddaughter left for a firm closer to her home in New Hampshire.

The new owner, an investor from the Midwest, decided to make the firm as profitable as possible by both growing the assets of the firm under management and making certain that any inefficiencies in the back office operations were eliminated. A new partner was added who later became the acting CEO in 1996. His role was to bring in new managers to grow the business. He did this very well, and the addition of new managers added a depth to the investment team and resulted in considerable revenues. But the managers who were added were not team players since they had been recruited separately and brought with them their books of assets from other firms. This proved to be a difficult management challenge as the firm continued to grow and again change hands.

After about five years, in late 1998, the Midwest investor felt the stock market was strong and the time was ripe to sell the profitable firm and retire himself to Europe. This left the partner/CEO to continue to run the organization and help with any transition to new management. While the first sale from Patrick Williams to the investor had gone relatively smoothly, the second sale from the investor to a new set of investors turned out to be a bit more difficult. The sale was a successful one for the investor. He made a good profit on the sale and left within weeks for his new life. The CEO was left with new owners who he was unfamiliar with, and a group of staff, some of whom were just becoming adjusted to life without the Williams family in charge of the firm.

The new owners were basically financial owners. They bought the firm with a great deal of debt and placed the debt onto the firm. The firm retained its name of Patrick Williams and Associates, but it now was part of a large conglomerate of companies owned by the financial group. This organization was not interested in the details of the money management business itself but was rather interested in the profits or losses of the company and was looking to manage it to be sold in a five-year time horizon. They assigned a person from their organization to oversee the financial matters of the firm and gave this person power to ask for and get any and all financial data needed for the financial conglomerate to manage the firm. Day-to-day management decisions were given over to the new CEO (John Jacobs) they hired. The current CEO who was the partner of the investor who sold the firm, became the Chairman, and agreed to stay on to help manage the firm.

The situation was a challenging one. The debt on the firm made running it very stressful. With a great deal of debt, the once debt-free and profitable firm began to feel pinched for cash and unable to spend as they wanted to gain new clients or upgrade the infrastructure. Eventually some funds were infused into the firm but it was not easy making this happen. The financial owners did not seem to want to fund the firm whose business they continued to misunderstand and mismanage.

Meanwhile, John Jacob attempted to manage the firm in ways that alienated people. He became occupied with doing deals that would bring new organizations into the firm to grow its capacity. While this effort for the most part did not work, one major acquisition did add a new office and capacity, but the manager there proved difficult to please and would not integrate with the rest of the firm. This made other efficiencies hoped for with the acquisition impossible.

Within a year, John was found seriously wanting among his own financial group. He was fired and the search was on for a new CEO. The firm began to suffer from the combination of new owners and a CEO (John) who hadn't lasted too long. People who had been part of a very stable and slow growth company found themselves concerned that these new financial owners were not only not an improvement over the first owner, but rather a much worse alternative. Although not all the employees understood the problems of the high levels of debt, many of the money managers did. This served to undermine their confidence in the firm.

Don Marshall, the new CEO, proved to be the final disaster for the financial owners. Don came from Maryland with an outstanding record of managing big firms and growing them successfully. However, his experience running complex and large organizations with large staffs did not prepare him to run a small and highly independent group of money managers who felt they owned their own clients and had little need for supervision. Continuing to worry about debt, they now felt overburdened by Don who set out to "organize" and systematize the organization. He added new marketing staff—a risky and expensive move—and attempted to reorder the firm from one of collegial interactions to more formal meetings, structure, and procedures. Although initially some decided to give Don a chance, this CEO's tenure was quite unpleasant for most at the firm, and often counterproductive.

Meanwhile, the financial owners began to feel anxious. They had bought the firm and placed great debt on it. They had hoped that John Jacob would manage deals and grow them into prosperity. But between market changes and the failure of this strategy for growth, they wasted several years. Don was not producing fast enough with his marketing team that took time to grow and his structuring ideas to satisfy them. With the Chairman trying hard to keep folks together and motivated, and the declining health of the stock market itself, things were not looking good. For the first time many of the employees of Patrick Williams were worried and concerned about the future and what would become of the firm if Don's plans did not work out—and they did not look promising.

More pressures to perform were put on the firm and this, along with cuts in all expenses, made many unhappy as well as frightened. All through these times, the performance record of the money managers was good if not great, considering the tough market conditions. But these good results were not enough to help continue to grow the firm at the same rate or add new customers fast enough to make up for the poor decisions the owners and its management team had put into place. Frustrated, the owners started shopping the firm by 2002. A new owner was eventually found in 2003 and Patrick Williams, once again in a period of 10 years, was sold—this time to another investor from London who bought the firm for cash and eliminated the debt. This new owner is just beginning his work at Patrick Williams. For the most part, few were sorry to see Don and his unsuccessful marketing team leave. The strategy had seemed flawed to most and his emphasis on systems above a collegial atmosphere was not the style most wanted at Patrick Williams. The firm is now attempting to regain its culture of shared and open communication and ownership in the future. A temporary President from the money managers has been chosen to lead while the company's future is being thought through.

At this point it is too early to tell if a new management can regain some of the good feelings that were present when the company was first sold in 1993, which was a smart sale that seemed to energize an aging firm. But the next sale to the financial owners seems to have undone much of the progress that was made. It is now up to the new owners to set a fresh vision and direction for the company, ensure that the entire staff understands it, and that they are on board to create a positive future. Without a good deal of mutual dialogue and input of all the employees and a strong vision and good leadership, Patrick Williams is going to continue to struggle to find its true spot in the competitive but ever-promising world of money management.

We thought that Patrick Williams, although filled with sophisticated people, might not do as well as other firms since they had simply been through too much change in a relatively short time. We were also worried that poor leadership may have affected people's perceptions of the value of changes.

Table 27. Mean Scores on the Change Reaction Scale for Patrick Williams and Associates (n=14) Compared to All Respondents (n=642)

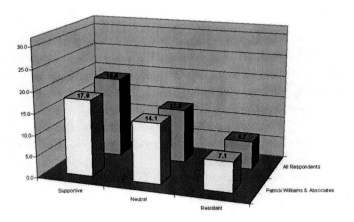

Table 28. Mean Scores on the Emotional Competence Inventory for Patrick Williams and

Associates (n=14) Compared to All Respondents (n=642)

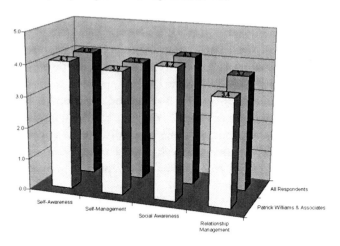

Commentary:

Looking at the change resistance tool scores, it becomes clear that our fears were somewhat well-founded. Patrick Williams had among the most resistant scores and the lowest supportive scores toward change. We see this as a direct result of changes that were instituted that subsequently did not go as planned, or in a positive direction.

In terms of EI, the scores remained primarily high, which demonstrates personal maturity on the part of the group. The one low area was relationship management, and a closer look suggested conflict management was a concern. We again saw this as consistent with the issues and problems of the organization. The management was sometimes detached from the staff as they were working on changes, and this led to internal conflicts that were not always handled smoothly. It is interesting, however, that despite the issues and problems, the overall profile of the people at Patrick Williams was higher in three of the four clusters of EI. Tough times did not affect the overall positive EI of these people.

Special Group Administration, Federal Government

The mission of the Special Group Administration, in partnership with other administrative groups of government, is to provide benefits and services to individuals with special needs and their families in a responsive, timely, and compassionate manner.

Their web site clearly states their mission. "Our vision is that the special group that we serve will feel that our nation has kept its commitment to them, employees will feel that they are both recognized for their contribution and are part of something larger than themselves, and taxpayers will feel that we've met the responsibilities they've entrusted to us. Courage, honesty, trust, respect, open communication, and accountability will be reflected in our day-to-day behavior."

The web site further states its core values in great detail which included the following points. First, that their special group deserves respect and that they are the reason for the existence of this government entity. All efforts are geared to making certain the special group is served and served well. Other core values include being professional, accurate, understandable, and respectful. Integrity, trust, and fairness, as well as openness to change and flexibility, are all important to this agency, which is focused on servicing its special needs group at the highest levels of professionalism.

The leadership pledge, clearly front and center on the web site, provides the spirit of the agency. "We, the undersigned, accept accountability, embrace integrity, and commit to exhibiting professionalism in the execution of our mission of service to our special needs group. In all of our action, we pledge to be guided by these fundamental principles of leadership, thereby ensuing fulfillment of this covenant."

The group, which responded to our survey, is one of five departments scattered around the United States who provide technology support to the main agency. Because this agency has been part of the government for many years, elections do not seem to create enormous amounts of change, although occasionally federal issues such as Clinton's battle with the house over funding, did somewhat effect the workings of the agency.

In general, this group, as all government groups, has been affected by the smaller government push since the early 1980s. Downsizing has been a consistent feature of government life, and this group has been no exception. The chain of command has grown, as has the use of outside contractors who receive higher pay. Some, of course, resent these higher paid contractors while others see them as a fact of life and treat them as colleagues. We saw this as one of our red flag issues, since downsizing nearly always causes some discomfort and the hiring of outside contractors is often a hot button issue for staff.

The executive we spoke with felt that part of his job was keeping people calm and focused. He felt he did that and for the most part people were not that anxious about downsizing. However, people do understand that there is constant pressure to keep costs down.

The relationship with the customers of the organization was described as good to very good. This group interacts with those who are on the front lines, working directly with the special needs group the agency serves. This middle group of customers used to be made up of only other government colleagues but has grown to include outside groups such as financial institutions who then in turn serve the ultimate group. These newer relationships are going particularly well, which was a point of pride to the executive to whom we spoke.

As with many other government agencies, the issue of baby boomer retirement looms. Many are looking ahead to retirement and this sometimes clashes with the need for the continued use of new and better technology. But some people are actually excited by and challenged by the new opportunities to learn, while others find the new technology too overwhelming and something to be avoided. This is a balancing act that this executive is dealing with daily.

Newer and younger workers seem interested in moving up, which is a good thing. The dot.com bubble and subsequent downturn has given many younger people who may have thought a career in the government would be uninteresting or low-paying time to reconsider and determine that it might be a job worth pursuing. Younger people are in fact staying, and turnover among this group as with the group at large is low.

The government is aware of the need to keep the best people and is attempting to offer more incentives, including repayment of some student loans and providing challenging technology work. Overall, this appears to be working. As noted, this is important since there will be a loss of knowledge and increased positions needing to be filled by those who want a career when the boomer group leaves the workforce.

The issues of change facing this group are primarily process improvements, including implementing change management with a new technology tool called Dimensions. Also, improving documentation and implementing project management will be of concern. Increased technical testing with the use of new automated tools are also important changes. These changes can all be seen as part of an overall increased understanding of and interest in creating a more defined and successful software process improvement culture that is totally embraced and consistently applied. These efforts have driven other changes and challenges such as the need for more training in new technologies mentioned above. This suggested to us another red flag—although these types of changes are generally well received, they can also unnerve people who worry that they cannot keep up or stay current with all the needed changes. This pressure can sometimes make for nervous and slightly disgruntled staff.

It appears that changes will continue to be part of this group's environment as it faces more standards, procedures, and tools to make QA a part of doing business all the time. The executive we spoke to felt confident that things were going in the right direction and that the organization for the most part was clearly on the right path. Although the government might well be more like a business in its efforts for quality and cost consciousness, these types of changes did not appear to be harmful, but rather helping the special needs group to increase its productivity and its ability to attract and retain new workers.

Table 29. Mean Scores on the Change Reaction Scale for Special Group Administration, Federal

Government (n=30) Compared to All Respondents (n=642)

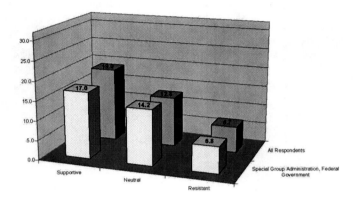

Table 30. Mean Scores on the Emotional Competence Inventory for Special Group

Administration (n=30) Compared to All Respondents (n=642)

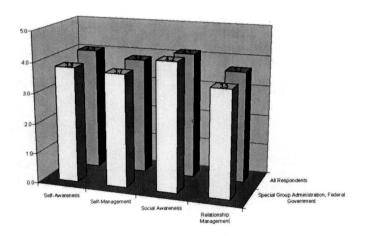

Commentary:

The scores on the change reaction tool were lower than we even predicted. Like Patrick Williams, it does appear that all the changes in the organization impacted people to have less support and higher resistance to change. Although not terrible scores, our government workers seemed to be feeling a bit more negative toward some of the changes they were experiencing.

In terms of EI, the government workers held their own with scores nearly identical to the total group. Although very slightly lowered in relationship management, their scores were statistically identical to those of the total group. In other words, they too were a highly emotionally intelligent group, who although not always positive to every change, seemed able and willing to deal with change effectively.

CHAPTER 11

Conclusion

Phase two of the research was designed to delve deeper into sites and situations to determine if specific work conditions and/or leadership and culture issues would demonstratively help or hinder people's scores in change reaction and EI.

Our overall finding is quite simple and dramatic. Although we might like to believe all these factors are critical, in our research the changes that were due to the specifics in a given situation were relatively minor. We did see the most swings in the change reaction tool. In this case, organizations that were more pro-change had leaders handling change deftly, and were going in a more positive direction clearly had staff who were more positive and less resistant toward change.

But, in terms of EI, most people held their own in terms of their high scores and appeared even with somewhat tough situations or relatively poor leadership to be emotionally mature and stable in their EI scores. This confirmed our phase one findings that people are far from change adverse, but in fact are both highly pro-change, open to change, and emotionally intelligent enough to handle change. In fact, when we had concerns about rapid change, as in the case of Visual Technologies, scores on both change reaction and EI were high. Federal government workers were no less mature in their EI than Wall Street executives and technology workers. The forces of globalization, along with changes in the overall economy and culture, seem to have given people the belief that change and growth are critical to their success even under difficult and challenging situations.

Our phase two research did support our selection of four pro-change and four mixed bag sites—but by a hair, and a case could be made that the differences were so slight as to be unimportant or inconsequential. But the data demonstrates, if only in a minor way, that leadership remains key and that specific situations do affect people. The good news is that people handle even relatively poor situations better than we might suppose and are ready and willing to give themselves to reinvention and change with direction from leadership. Rather than worrying about people's resistance, the wise leader is moving ahead quickly, and employees appear more than ready to grasp the opportunity to make the necessary changes.

PART IV

Recommendations for Action

SYNOPSIS AND IMPLICATIONS

When we discovered that people were more pro-change than neutral or negative, we thought through what that meant in terms of policies and processes of handling change initiatives. We also considered what knowing that most people are willing to listen and are open to being influenced meant in terms of leadership and management behaviors. Finally we thought about what it would mean for individuals. In each case there were numerous implications. For example, if you have a majority of people already pro any reasonable change, why spend time with big meetings that are designed to get people excited about change? They already are, but the devil is in the details—so logically we would recommend more time on those details and more time getting people involved and engaged rather than convinced of the need for change. They likely will GET IT quickly but want to see details and get deeper into the problems, challenges, and what the options are for moving forward.

The problem with recommendations of any kind is that they can sound or seem obvious or trite on one hand, or be perceived as a stretch from the data on the other hand. Our decision was to include in our recommendations those things that are not just common sense or common knowledge, or even best practices, but ideas that make sense due to the data we collected and thoughtfully analyzed. We discovered a much stronger pro-change bias than we thought in people. We therefore suggest that less time and effort be spent at all levels discussing the need to change and many more opportunities for inclusion in making things change. This may be one of those ideas that appears "obvious." But is it?

How often, even in today's sophisticated organizations, do you find that change initiatives are limited to small groups of people making decisions for the majority? How often do you see people at high levels continuing to make it obvious to people in the ranks that they do not know what is going on or what would be a better approach? In another instances, we may know it is a "best practice" to involve people, but now we know for certain, at least with our research subjects, that not only is that a good idea but a necessary idea and even wasteful and fruitless to do otherwise.

On the individual level we suggest things that are based on the research into people's emotional intelligence and change reaction and the Big Picture information we gleaned. For instance, we mention travel as a good idea especially for the young and unencumbered—again, perhaps an obvious tip for those in their formative years. If our research is to be believed, this isn't just a good coming of age idea, it may be an absolute for survival and understanding the changing dimensions of the global economy. While we tried not to stretch the data too much, we did suggest that any efforts to think women might be more open to change, or younger groups more easy to work with on change initiatives would in light of our research not be wise. We do not believe this is the commonsense thinking out there. As consultants, we often hear ideas that "our older employees are more resistant than our younger ones"—well not according to our research. We also did not find differences by job categories, though we did not discuss this at length in the research findings. In fact, we did find many differences once we were in organizations on any demographic characteristics. This is in our view an interesting finding and makes our recommendations applicable for any types of workers of any age in a wide range of organizations.

One of the most important ideas that we present in our recommendations is our belief that the time is now right for the Learning Organization—a term and strategy popularized nearly 15 years ago and lost in the shuffle of change strategies and the poor economy. The emotional intelligence data we found supports the idea that the time may be right for the successful implementation of the learning organization strategy. While the idea of a learning organization might have been premature some number of years ago, times have changed as well as people—and with higher levels of emotional intelligence, the tools and processes of creating a learning organization might well be possible now when it was not just five or less years ago.

We thought about our data, we talked about it, and then we selected ideas and presented in Chapter 12 as "Ins" and "Outs" for each relevant group—individuals, leaders, and organizations. The chapter that follows crystallized the main ones we developed. But for sure, the list is incomplete. The research we undertook and analyzed gives rise to many more ideas than we present. However, those would likely best be discovered organization by organization. We encourage dialogue at every level. In fact, this book, whether read in the short form (just the synopsis of each part and this chapter) or in its entirety, should generate discussion in any organization about how it is that workers with higher levels of thinking and more positive attitudes toward change can help create the organizations of the future.

CHAPTER 12

Making Meaning from Research

When we began the journey of understanding the world of work post 9/11, we really were not sure what we would find, but we had hunches as all researchers do. Our initial thinking and experiences at work created an impression employees were evolving. We knew we ourselves had been impacted by trends of culture, terrorism, and of course globalization, and thought others likely had been as well. Despite the Bush re-election that on the surface indicated a strong right shift in thinking, we thought people, regardless of who they voted for, were really broader thinkers than the media suggested. We perceived people as more open to new ideas whether left or right—in fact wishing and hoping for MORE from both sides of the aisle.

Something about the whole campaign of 2004 struck us as not being "what it seemed" on the surface. Current trends seem to support our thinking that the harsh divide and the whole red state/blue state implication of simple thinking is getting more "fuzzy" now. Majorities of citizens of all types were in favor of the mixed group of senators who brokered a compromise in the senate, did not interfere in the Terri Schiavo case, increased expansion of stem cell research, and even protected major elements of social security or considered new and unique ideas to preserve its core while allowing differences going forward. This suggests to us not right or wrong or left or right thinking, but nuanced thinking that indicates a higher level of reasoning and a more mature approach to world events and issues of the day. Simple black and white is not resonating with the public, whose views are more thoughtful and balanced in most cases. This is a good thing in an increasingly complex world.

Our hunches were telling us, despite the words of many managers and leaders, that people were anti-change and difficult to deal with around changing strategies, and that somehow people were evolving. But how? And why were so many managers and leaders missing this shift if, in fact, there was one? Was the organizational change literature and much of what was being preached starting with assumptions that people were change adverse and simple thinkers? Was that advice wrong or based on old, outdated and now false assumptions? Or were people more change adverse than we thought, and our hunches about their evolving was really just wishful thinking?

We felt that our experiences at companies where we were meeting new young global executives were "telling us" that people at work were maturing and open, although as we observed, not always well-led and managed. We knew too that many we worked with and interacted with had subtly shifted gears, with their "rudders" more firmly going toward the personal and the familial.

It seemed that "suddenly" (although it was far from suddenly, more like an evolution), in a vastly more complicated and competitive world, lots of people at work no longer worried about what colleagues thought about their commitment—they thought about and proudly proclaimed that the most important people in their lives were not their employers or their customers, but their families. We knew we were a long way from the 1980s pervasive preoccupation with career and the 1990s preoccupation with money and success, even though money traditionally defined success, and security ironically was more important than ever to protect one's self, one's family, and one's home. Neither careerism nor materialism has gone away. Both are still ongoing, major factors in the workplace, but there has been a significant shift in that work has definitively taken a back seat to family and security concerns (in the broadest sense of those words) in the United States.

Could this shift toward family concerns and desire for balance in life be what some leaders and managers were seeing as a shift right, and an anti-change or lack of flexibility toward change at work? Could be. We didn't know. We also thought it was interesting to observe the family shift, in light of what is happening globally and economically. In some ways, without looking too deeply, it might appear that we in the United States are out of step with others globally. Since so many outside the United States are now scrambling to get on the fast track economically, while many here might appear to be trying to get off that track. We don't believe that is at all the case. Yes, Americans are shifting toward family and deeper personal meaning, but by no means are they less interested in work and progress and competing. What they want is a change in the processes of work and the way work is done. They hunger, it seems to us, for better leadership (politically, religiously, and locally as well as work) and acceptance of new realities while balancing the needs for deep change at work to keep competitive.

For those in war-torn areas around the world, of course security remains logically the most fundamental need, want, and necessity. But, with those global economic giants China and India, the scene looks much like the United States a few years ago, when getting up the ladder was the most prominent focus. This makes sense in light of current realities explained so beautifully by the brilliant work of Thomas Friedman's *The World Is Flat: A Brief History of the Twenty-first Century* (2005). While it is clear that most if not all people put family first, the times and new opportunities allow people to be more involved with work and careers than others who may have long had opportunities to make a living and secure a future for themselves and their families.

CHANGE AHEAD

In Mr. Friedman's insightful book on where the world is "right now" in terms of globalization, he explains the ten key technology and economic events that have collaboratively created the conditions for the current phase of globalization, or what he calls Globalization 3.0. He suggests this particular phase is flattening or leveling the playing field, allowing individuals to compete. "Around 2000 we entered a whole new era: Globalization 3.0. Globalization 3.0 is shrinking the world from a size small to a size tiny and flattening the playing field at the same time. And while the dynamic force in Globalization 1.0 was countries globalizing, and the dynamic force in Globalization 2.0 was companies globalizing, the dynamic force in Globalization 3.0—the thing that gives it its unique character—is the newfound power for individuals to collaborate and compete globally." (page 10)

His insights into people striving to share in the riches and prosperity of this phase of globalization demonstrates conclusively that there will never be a shortage of those whose primary focus, from this period of time forward for the foreseeable future, is getting on board with opportunities previously denied them. And, these people will increasingly be nonwestern and nonwhite. At the same time, it's likely a lesser number of people will be striving to find deeper meaning and security once they have become established or at least consider themselves somewhat secure (a likely unhealthy and unrealistic point of view for most), due to the successes previous/current globalization has afforded them.

It makes sense to us that those who have had so much relative success (and then experienced a terrific act of terror such as 9/11 or 7/7) might stop to reflect on what is MOST meaningful in life and to conclude it is one's own deepest yearnings, and of course, one's family. It also makes complete sense to us that those who have never had the chance to savor opportunities will quickly take up the slack that any nonattention to new opportunities allows them—not as an anti-American move, but in a pro-themselves desire to provide for their own yearnings and families. This is reassuring, and for some who are insecure about their own ability to compete in a new flattened world, frightening. Since loss is a necessary component of any type of growth, the issue of coping and coping well comes down to a belief that even with loss comes something better or at least as good. And, that this growth and change is part of life and inevitable.

Acceptance of loss and growth is something that our evolving culture has both made more palatable and more acceptable. In Chapter 1 we talked about the changing culture and the openness to growth that it implies and supports. From Oprah to Dr. Phil, from new spirituality to increased emphasis on health and fitness, people are exposed to the idea that change does mean work, loss, and upheaval, but it also brings rewards as well as different and new opportunities. How can this persuasive culture NOT have some impact on personal change—and hence workplace change—in many Americans? If change is good and necessary, then logically change and growth at work and in our organizations is necessary too.

At the same time that evolving technology has allowed for new members on the world economic playing field, we see examples of how the older developed nations such as the United States (though we are lagging, we are still in the mix here) are working on issues of deeper meaning and values. Diverse groups including but not limited to conservative Jews and Christians, and entertainers like Bono, have impacted the decisions of the "have nations" to forgive "lesser developed/third world" debt, and to consider a serious new and revised attack on African poverty.

These efforts, spurred by new thinking of the United Nations with its millennium goals and economists like Jonathan Sacks, suggest that while the world is adding many to share in the pie, some are working to make certain that as time progresses more and more will be able to get into the picture and participate in the expanding global economy. Along this same line, we observe vast new sums being pledged by those like Bill Gates and his wife Melinda Gates who have reaped the blessings and rewards of previous economic opportunities. This suggests that in many ways, the haves and have-nots, and the "almost haves" in places like India and China, who may appear to be in a different psychological or philosophical place, are really in the same place. They are participating in the flattening world that is furthering connection, increasing opportunities for all peoples, and yet allowing those who have had success to continue to be successful if they participate in the shifting economy.

While the old idea of the haves and have-nots assumed a limited pie and a world view that some must have at the expense of others who have not, we see a new world view, based on new opportunities that suggests that if all have or if more have, everyone is better off. We are essentially creating new, bigger pies that create new opportunities. Again, this can be seen as either good or frightening news. And, the broader thinking one has, the more open to change, and the more willing to concede that change brings a different life as well as necessary losses, the more willing one is to participate in one's own growth, leading to growth at work.

We continued to observe that the United States workforce was shifting, that there were more pressures from global competition, but what more was going on with the workforce and how could that help or hinder the efforts of organizations and individuals needing to change gears or transform? Were we foolish Pollyannas with an unrealistic view of working people and progress, or were we observing a genuine shift of thinking?

The world is flat—the playing field is opening and continuing to open to many previously excluded. While some who "owned" opportunities might now have more competition, it is hard for those who fought for opportunity themselves (such as most working Americans) to discourage others from doing the same once change makes it possible. This means that although there will be some attempts to limit globalization, especially by those with vested interests in some status quo, and to retain what some see as our deserved and rightful pre-eminence in the world, most United States workers will embrace globalization as they increasingly understand its positive implications for themselves, and accept their own responsibility to live with new realities that can, if properly handled, allow for a different, more flattened world with unique new opportunities for themselves as well as new entrants to the world's stage.

The world has continued to shift and change as Mr. Friedman and others explain. And our attempt to understand people's changes of mind were happening at the same time that the forces Mr. Friedman observed were happening. We were pondering what was on people's minds post 9/11, and we were wondering if people "had what it takes" to deal with the myriad changes going on in the world. We did NOT have a clear understanding of what Mr. Friedman called Globalization 3.0, and neither did Mr. Friedman, who concedes he was otherwise engaged with his post 9/11 attempt to understand the Muslim world and help others understand those dynamics.

Both phases of our research demonstrated strongly and conclusively, that people had been deeply affected by the change in our culture and world since 9/11. Unlike the issue of Globalization 3.0, which many likely have not even begun to grasp or fully consider, people did know about 9/11 and reacted to it. The greatest shift post 9/11 appears to be a new sense on the part of working Americans of meaning and commitment to oneself to do what one can to value what people know are their most important treasures, and to work to make certain their futures to the extent they could control them, are secure. Whether people have successfully implemented actions to create that security is in doubt with increased personal debt and less savings, but we sense that even with all the bad news and likely poor strategy or execution in those regards, people are both seeking solutions and working to secure the road ahead.

In terms of work, we saw several strong trends that bode well once people DO start to grasp more fully the changing world of work and the implications for themselves and their work due to Globalization 3.0. First and foremost, our sample in phase two was highly emotionally intelligent. They demonstrated strong skills in the four areas of emotional intelligence—self-awareness, self-management, social awareness, and relationship management.

Although some conditions and situations in our sites created some minor shifts in the levels of emotional intelligence, those shifts were very slight and statistically rather insignificant. Further, we saw that despite other research on generations at work or genders in the workplace, our participants did not vary by any outward difference such as age or gender. People at work at this time seem to clearly have the emotional capacity to deal with changes as well as to lead them. We did not, of course, find perfectly emotionally intelligent people, but without exception, scores were above average and strongly suggestive of positive attitudes toward maturity in terms of handling change and growth. This is nothing but great news given increasing competition, the fact that managers and leaders are not always as competent as they might be, and the urgent need for organizations of every stripe to transform to compete in the new century.

A bit more of a mixed picture emerged in terms of reactions to change. Most people were strongly pro-change personally—but at work, it did vary just a bit. Differences in specific work situations and leadership influenced scores on the Change Reaction Tool, creating either more outright resistance to change efforts or more neutral stances toward it. This too made sense to us, but is troubling for organizations with weaker leadership or no concrete and viable plans to strengthen leadership. With practical concerns of family, values, and meaning front and center for workers in the United States, people can be cautious in their attitudes to change. But they are not by any means adverse to it or "worried about it" in the sense that they are naïve or unrealistic about what is happening or will happen as the world economy evolves. With the right leadership, information (which they are increasingly getting even without help and guidance from their leadership), and support, our strongly emotionally intelligent workforce can and will cope with and survive and thrive in these strongly competitive and challenging times.

Our research can give hope to individuals, managers and leaders, and organization boards and key executives who are wondering how in the world they can deal with new realities and their workforce. The workforce is ready, willing, and able if there is respect for them as individuals, if their families and priorities are considered and understood, and if the leadership of organizations allows an adult conversation and involvement of people in leading their own futures.

These are tall orders, but doable. They do not, however, rest on the assumptions of most current business people who seem stuck in the flawed assumptions of people from earlier times. As Stephen Covey suggests in his masterful follow-up to the *Seven Habits of Highly Effective People: Powerful Lessons in Personal Change* (1989) called *The 8th Habit: From Effectiveness to Greatness* (2004), leaders today are clearly working with old, outdated assumptions of how organizations and people work. People have essentially moved beyond the thinking of most leaders and managers. While managers and leaders themselves are more sophisticated in their thinking, as were their colleagues, they appear to persist in believing in the un-evolved and the less than pro-change thinkers of old. Old style management and leadership despite the enormous literature base that suggests it is dumped in favor of more enlightened approaches, just is not reaching far and wide enough to support the changes we or Dr. Covey see in the workforce.

The Internet, technology more broadly, and the open culture of the United States with its support of personal change and growth has moved the average individual ahead of the leadership curve. Add in the realities of a post 9/11 world, we have a nation of empowered individuals of every type and persuasion. As Thomas Friedman put it, the time for individuals is NOW. "Individuals must, and can now ask, where do I fit into the global competition and opportunities of the day, and how can I, on my own, collaborate with others globally?" (Page 10) Our research data suggests that this is a question that many are "getting" and "answering," and that if organizations and its leaders are wise, they will fully grasp and incorporate this understanding into their own thinking about how to work with employees of every level and type moving forward.

Although many may appear on the surface to be "lost at sea," do not know whether the world is flat, round, or what the world has to do with them anyhow, our subjects, taken from both a broad open survey and from a variety of types and styles of organizations, HAVE GOTTEN IT. They know they need to change, they know they need to grow, and they know that life as we know it is never going to get easier, simpler, or more parochial. Just as the media (and some religious and other leaders) underestimated where people's thinking is and was politically—missing the complexity of thought and the gray that most people see, feel, and understand—most managers and leaders are missing the fact that people in organizations GET IT and don't need to be patronized, talked down to, and brought kicking and screaming to deal with the realities of Globalization 3.0 or any other economic reality. They understand they need to change—what they are looking for is help with HOW to change, WHAT to do, and how best to compete moving forward. The self-help gurus of every type and persuasion are giving advice on everything from diet to managing one's money. Leaders need to get on board with a plan of action, jointly developed with sophisticated workers, that outlines where next to deal with the realities of the economic world. Don't worry that people are change adverse, worry about how to move ahead.

People know they have to change—they need to grow and they need to perform at high levels to achieve or even to remain financially stable. How could they have missed that message given the history of the stock market, evolving times, and government messages of impending gloom on the health care and retirement fronts? People do not expect things to be easy, simple, or routine, and they are ready with the right leadership to do what it takes because most are grounded, informed, and aware, as well as spiritually and emotionally focused on their family and their own survival.

As consultants, we never feel good about just understanding situations. We want to help, advise, counsel, and support change and growth that builds on what we know. Since we have this research, we want to use it to suggest what strategies and approaches to personal and organizational change and transformation that make sense in light of this new knowledge. The remainder of this chapter suggests ideas for individuals, leaders, and organizations that are attempting to deal with change effectively. We are now going to answer this question: "If what we found is true—that people are changed post 9/11 (not all, but many) and people are both more open to change and emotionally intelligent than we thought, what are the implications of this research for individuals, leaders, and organizations going forward?" We also touch on those strategies and approaches based on our research that are less effective going forward.

For each group we will list what is "in" and what is "out" in terms of perceptions, approaches, and useful strategies for the world of work. While many of these ideas are not new, or even unique, they are not in common practice or widely accepted. Nor previous to our work were they placed in a research context that suggests people have the wherewithall to handle and accept them. We end with the hope that this book will be an addition to the thinking, planning, and understanding of individuals and leaders engaged with organizational change and transformation in the 21st century.

Collectively, we can all make a leap forward—and make more progress than ever thought possible if we agree to agree that the world has changed—and thankfully, most people know it and are open to it at least those working, those plugged into technology, and those interacting in the workplace. Unfortunately, we are aware this leaves some people out.

Although there are those who are "out of it," which our research suggests is a smaller group than imagined, focusing on the small minority is not a good strategy for the vast majority of organizations. Focusing on the minority is important for the government in terms of preserving rights. It is not the best course of action for changing a company or a foundation, or a mosque or church, in the 21st century. Organizational change posits a good greater than any one individual. It purports that its mission and vision serves a greater good and does not exist for specific people, but rather for those who can believe in and engage its mission and vision and make that mission and vision a reality for its customers and stakeholders. There is room for all individuals, just not in a given organization. This is an important and critical distinction.

As for individuals, it is our belief that those who are truly lost at sea would take a good deal more than a good book, any number of books, or even serious therapy to help wrestle them into understanding the reality of the 21st century with its challenges and opportunities. There are some, too, who lack the essential skills and mental abilities, the emotional intelligence, and/or the proper education, or are psychologically disadvantaged and unable to participate fully in these challenging times. We are counting on those professionals in government, education, social work, and even religious organizations to grapple with the future of these people who legitimately must participate in society, have opportunities commensurate with their strengths as well as disabilities, and be handled with dignity and find a secure place in this ever-changing and competitive world.

We in organizations can help by making every opportunity available to every person possible to enter into organizations and share in their resources—to find their strengths and needs and plug them into the vast web of the world where their talents, needs, desires, viewpoints, and life can best intersect with others of complementary type. But for the purposes of this book, we offer strategies to those who can see, hear, and understand what is going on in the world and accept the new realities to help them go to the next level of plugging into the future. In our mind, that future has few limits, lots of upside, tremendous opportunity, and looks to be in good hands with all the tremendously talented people developing and plugging in all over the world.

The Individual

Individuals are the new multinationals. They are the starting point of any venture and any opportunity. Where ten or twenty years ago no one person could get into the global economy and compete, now millions can, do, and will. Individuals need to be aware of their new power and understand the leverage they have IF they are plugged in, connected, and willing to participate in the new world. That said, the disempowered, the sad sack, the one looking for management to guide and save them, the one looking for the next Enron who might promise a bright future on air, or the next real estate boom that will make them rich for little or no effort, are essentially doomed to a go-slow or no-go lane of mediocrity. Of course there are many jobs available for the unfocused, the uninformed, and the want-to-be-led crowd. They just aren't particularly good, stable, or secure jobs, or jobs likely to provide secure futures and any real upward mobility.

The mantra for the individual now is: WAKE UP and CONTINUE to smell the coffee! We found most people were aware of the need to change, they just need to keep reminding themselves that this is not a mindless mantra, but a real and tangible need for each person to take it upon themselves to figure out what is going on in their particular field of endeavor, from carpeting manufacturing to high finance, from teaching to farming, from painting and classical music to entertainment management, from government technology work to insurance sales, no work, no job, no career is untouched by what is going on in the world economy, and smart, plugged-in workers are continually scanning the environment of their work world and learning about what it all means for them personally. They are reading, observing, looking at the wide view of everything happening to them as well as their competition—and that implies worldwide competition, their industry, their field, and digesting what this means in terms of opportunities and real and present threats as well. The individual of ANY level, in ANY field that is aware, plugged in, networked, and seeking to grow his or her own competencies, has opportunity; those that don't can take their chances. We would not suggest they do.

That said, what's IN for individuals in the workplace based on what we learned in our Big Picture, and phase one and two of our research?

- Since you know you accept change and need to change, why not let your management know that so they can stop thinking you don't want to change?
- Since you understand the need to change, why not be more proactive in helping your organization respond to the changes it needs to make—take charge and demonstrate that you do understand and accept the need for change that our research shows you have.
- If your family comes first be clear with others on how that effects them at work, be open about what the bottom line is for you—make it easy to manage you and figure out what you need to be satisfied. Make it easy, safe, and a plus to work with you, manage you, and help you contribute. No one has time for whiners anymore.
- Develop a current list of competencies needed in one's field NOW. These are often found on the sites of associations, among leaders in any industry group, or through one's own human resources department. If you work in a small shop of any type, look at industry newsletters, association publications, or leading organizations in your field. If you work for the leader, look within your own resources.
- Evaluate yourself against the trends. Are you keeping up or losing ground? Start getting serious about your own development. Here is when you can stop learning: the day you stop working forever and retire completely, permanently, and with no need to ever again (and we mean ever again!) do another lick of work for money.
- Ask for feedback all the time from your boss, your colleagues, and your customers. Know yourself and help others make it easy to tell you how you are doing. Many managers are poor at giving feedback and avoid it—you have to ask or you won't get the input you need. Trust us.
- Since management often thinks that older people (that's over 30), men, or certain less educated groups are more resistant to change than our research found them to be, then make sure if you are in one of these groups you let the management know you are on the pro-change side—our research suggests you are more emotionally intelligence and more pro-change—let people know that about you.
- If you have no clue what you want to do, we suggest you find your passion and explore the field thoroughly then get into something—anything. We do not believe anyone reading this book would not have at least one passion or interest. Planning without getting involved is not going to help. It

is much easier to move within an industry than to get into it. Do whatever it takes to get into the field that you are passionate about, then network, build relationships, learn, grow, and move. Stop looking for the right opportunity, go for any opportunity then grow.

- If you need to make money, think multiple paths and think outside your normal ideas of what is acceptable. With everyone focused on his or her own lives, no one cares what you are doing. If people at the club/old neighborhood/right neighborhood don't approve, and you care, you are asking the wrong question and going about the "work/career thing" all wrong. It is not a contest or a race—it is part of living and making a life. Doing what you have to do to survive makes sense, caring what the "Joneses" think or anyone thinks went out with the old style Oldsmobile some of our fathers drove. It is an ineffective use of limited energy, better spent figuring out what is going on in the world and participating. In a simpler time, we could waste some time "idling"—we don't have that luxury anymore. Our research suggests people want more time for themselves—don't waste any time as a means of preserving what you have for productive endeavors.

- If you are really young, then travel and see the world and what's going on first hand. You will never be the same, and good for you—you will be ahead of us all. My mother told me in the 1950s that travel was the best education. Mom was right.

- Do not hold out for the opportunity, but rather seek to look outside the usual to get the resources you need to live—if not well, at least to survive while you continue to seek other opportunities that you maybe never thought of before. Use the Internet to look on the fringe of your industry to see what's coming. And network with folks in your industry. But, since people are time conscious based on our research, be specific about the help you need and get to the point with people. People don't have the leisure they used to at work—and so speed of request is of the essence. Thank you's and handwritten responses have not gone out of style and are still hugely appreciated. Try sending a few and see what happens.

- Reach out and connect with people you never thought of connecting with—it is easier than ever, and more than ever before you will find people responding to you just because it is easy and they can. Don't be afraid of trying the old usual in new ways—the old school—even high school and grade school friends might be resources for new ideas and opportunities, and they want to pay you back for eating their donut in 4th grade. But again, thinking that people are concerned with their own issues, be brief and feel out the individual and their willingness to connect with you. The easier you make it—say by email, the easier it will be for them to openly respond to you.

- Don't focus on credentials without thinking how the network or skills you will gain will help you contribute to your customers and your field. Lots of people you never dreamed would have the same or better credentials than you will have them, so you better be able to add value or your credentials won't get you anywhere—and quickly. This was clear from our research on the big picture. People are getting the same credentials, and those in the U.S. are getting them faster—this trend will continue.

- The ability to work on a team and collaborate is the most important skill you need now. Better get cracking on figuring out how to get better at it. Practice anywhere you can, from politics, to church, to local community work, to family picnics. Research shows the most important thing in business is to get along and contribute to making teams work. Can't do it? A loner? Good luck. Hope you win the lottery.

- Diversity isn't just about (or really even about) black and white or male and female anymore. Realize diversity is in ideas, thoughts, perspectives, and a host of areas beyond race and gender. Hone your ability to listen, connect with, and work effectively with those different than yourself—and see the real value add in that. If you don't, our research suggests you might be left behind. And in the global economy, you will be quickly left behind. It was interesting that our research showed little to few differences among people due to differences of any outward type (gender, age, level in the organization)—this confirms in our mind that differences are everywhere, but no where obvious.

- If you think your work is local, or will not or cannot be effected by technology, you have to go back to the Internet and start reading and searching. Our data suggests others are doing it so you best get cracking. You are simply wrong that technology will not effect your work. Even if you are a waitress, an actor, a clerk in a store, or a house cleaner, or an accountant, lawyer, real estate agent, corporate something, or sales executive, you are really out of touch with reality. It is already happening.

- You have to be secure in yourself since the world offers both more opportunity and yet less security. You have to know yourself—really, not just the mask, or the superficial you. You have to work at these things since neither are easy nor come naturally for most people. While you are at it, help those you love to do these things—they are critical to their success too. The emotional intelligence results confirmed many are stronger here than we may have assumed. Keep at it.

- Risk is a good thing. Stupid risk isn't. If you don't know the difference, start thinking. Good risk—moving for a great job opportunity. Stupid risk—all your savings in a can't-lose, new business. Again, use the emotional intelligence data we saw.

What's OUT for individuals in the workplace?

- Saviors of any type—the CEO as hero and Goddess or God who will make it all work. Believing that what is happening to your industry, life, or business isn't fair or just. Wondering what happened while you were sleeping! This is again based on our Big Picture research as well as our research suggesting that change happens in organizations of all types with all levels.
- Secure career paths—any set career paths. If you build your own business or practice, who knows even then? Ask the self-employed how secure they feel.
- Security without lots of risk, especially if you're in a group enterprise versus a personal practice (like being a one-person attorney, doctor, or what not, and that is very tough and getting tougher and tougher...ask any one doing it).
- Thinking that your degree, background, or connections are all you need. Even Colin Hanks needs to be a great actor on his own, despite being Tom Hank's son.
- Not thinking someone else could do your job quicker, better, and more effectively than you do. If they aren't already, they will soon.
- Worrying rather than learning and growing.
- Not being a team player.
- Competing rather than collaborating.
- Looking to get over on people rather than looking to connect with your coworkers. Courtesy and connection are more vital than ever—and since many have good relationship skills and are practicing them according to our research, if you are not, you are going to be replaced.
- Thinking your workplace will stabilize at some point soon. No research supports this pipe dream.
- Thinking there is an end point; there is for you personally, but not your work or your organization's work.
- Trying to do things alone. Learning, growth, organizational change, successful enterprises, new product development, new markets, and successful stocks are all the result of team efforts. The only person who does things alone is a failure. Our research into change reactions suggests that most are willing and able to get involved with others to create and sustain change—if you are not in that group or team mindset others are and you will be left behind.
- Calm, dignified, peaceful, respectful, and practical conversations are NOT OUT—they are needed more than ever. We made a point earlier in the book of the need for leaders who can bring people together. The arrogant

have lost the race and destroyed good people and good businesses while destroying themselves. Don't ever believe the cynical individual or leader for one minute. They are usually the most scared and frightened people in the world. With high emotional intelligence more in practice only staff with greater levels of emotionally intelligence will progress up the ranks in most organizations.

In summary, it is a good time to be a strong, independent, and interdependent person with high emotional intelligence, guts, savvy, and openness to change and growth. It is a bad time to be scared, a loner, set in your ways, looking for the secure and stable route, or wondering when it is all going to stop moving so fast. It isn't going to. The great news is, the people we surveyed seem to have all the right stuff to succeed in this environment.

Managers and Leaders

As noted several times in this book, leaders and managers are getting lots of great advice, but they do not seem to be heeding it. We are not certain why that is. Perhaps it might be that despite the plethora of books, articles, and training available, only selected people are taking sufficient advantage of the knowledge out there and learning how best to use what is known about leadership and management to their advantage. It appears that organizations are not either providing the time to read and reflect on knowledge available, or making limited amounts of information available that they believe is sufficient for greater efficiency in their own organizations. Since poor leadership and management remains a problem and a challenge, we have to assume that not enough education is happening. This is a shame given that the guidance does exist, and in ways that is relatively inexpensive and painless.

One of the problems has been the lack of willingness of many organizations in tough times to sufficiently invest in their human resources. While organizations all claim people are their most important assets, most have yet to demonstrate that through consistent investments in people over other business investments, such as R&D or higher salaries for top officers. Similar to the mantra that our youth are our future, educational funding in organizations, like education in public life, is usually underfunded, lacking in the newest strategies, relegated to the bottom of priorities, and otherwise not focused on except in the literature of the HRD industry. We would like to think we are wrong here, but we often find that learning is not a strong priority or focus and generally there is hesitancy to spend in this area. The exceptions, of course, are the leading firms and leading countries whose belief in investment consistently pays off, but not immediately—a problem still for many organizations.

Our suggestions are simple really. Since this is the age of the individual, our data would urge managers and leaders to take every chance they have to push a learning agenda within their organizations. And certainly if you can or have the power to create any good decision, make it to invest in the knowledge expansion of your colleagues at work. But, after that, the best thing any leader or manager can do is to develop themselves based on the resources out there (and there are hundreds and thousands of them), to get better at leadership and better at managing.

What's In based on our research?
- Studying and training to be a leader like you train to keep your body in shape—all the time. Skipping development workouts does to your skills what not working out does to your body, it doesn't look good, does it?
- Observe the best leaders and managers in your organization, in your industry, and in other avenues in your life; identify them and emulate them. Study them like you would a great process. Don't mimic, emulate. You need to find your own voice as Stephen Covey says, but the essence of great leaders is the same.
- Read more than you want to about leadership. Skip the ones that have titles that use a warfare metaphor or imply sometime of head on aggressive approach. It is over for these types of strategies. The tough guy/tough woman act is amusing, except if you work for one of these fools of either sex. Don't believe what you see on reality TV. Work has no relationship to the nonsense of "you're fired" and other silly games of competition. It misses the whole point of modern business and organizational life. Our research into successful organizations, and our research into what people are thinking, strongly suggests that maturity and sophistication of thought as well as nuance and learning, rather than raw aggression, will win in today's organizations.
- Read more than you want to about management.
- If you can't manage, start there. Meaning, you have to be able to set goals, support and coach, motivate, create a fair environment, hire great people, help people out the door if they are the wrong fit, budget, guide, think big, collaborate with your colleagues, be part of the team, and lead it and all the other basics.
- Then, once capable, think bigger...to leadership. Leadership is based on emotional intelligence which we have found is growing. Be part of the vision, understand and communicate the mission and the vision, help people see the Big Picture, help create a positive and creative environment, support growth and change in others, don't ever be threatened by competence greater than your own. Support the best and make room for the best, keep the focus on the right things, not just doing things right.
- Get feedback on your management and leadership skills. Get it from those that know you best—those who work for you, those who interact with you,

and those who are from other departments or outside vendors, customers, or alliance partners who have to deal with your area. Of course your boss loves you, that is why you are there! Seriously, her view counts too, but likely you have that feedback even if you don't ask.

- Beware of complacency. If you read any of the synopsis you know how dangerous this is. Our research is overwhelming in making you avoid this one.
- Never think because you had success you will continue to be successful. With changes at warp speed, your past success just might be your undoing.
- Don't think you can get knocked off your perch? Have you read the papers lately? Hank Greenberg, Carly Fiorina, and even Philip Purcell with his board of cronies took the fall; likely you aren't in their world much less their net worth zone. Doesn't mean they might not reinvent themselves (or you couldn't). That is the best thing about the age we live in. Even Richard Nixon got another chance! If these names don't mean anything to you, maybe it is time to buy that subscription or go online to read the *Wall Street Journal.*
- Leaders should worry more about modeling what they want and less about what others aren't doing. This is especially important in light of the fact that more people are on board than you know. Paying too much attention to those not on board is not consistent with the implications of our research that suggests the strong majority are with you—go with them.
- Get a coach, even out of your own pocket. Like a work out coach, they push you.
- Get to know people as individuals, treat them as individuals, respect their uniqueness, and accept their reality of the world. They are your biggest assets, and their work (your collective work) depends on it being good for them, not just good for you. Go back to the section on the myth of change resistance if you have any doubt that people want and need to be recognized and seen as individuals.
- Go back and read the last point and memorize it. Do not under any circumstances forget it. We told you people are more self-focused. Believe it.
- Don't forget that lack of respect for someone is the surest way to get him/her to leave once they perceive there is any way out.

Out

- Thinking your people "don't get it." They do. You just don't know them well enough to figure out that they do. If information is out there anywhere, they know it. Google yourself and your company. Oh my. Did they have to put that out there?

- Thinking that you are smarter than other people. Even if you are, it won't last long. And besides, who really cares if you are so smart? The point of work of any kind, from medicine to plastics, is to solve problems, help customers, and do something of value…keep your eye on that ball. And, no work of ANY kind is ever done alone, so just think how you can help use your intelligence toward something. That's how you get "As" in life. Besides, if our data is correct, there are more smart people than ever—you are just one of many who really get it.
- Believing you can take credit for someone else's work. With the way technology works now it isn't going to happen, that went out with *My Little Margie* and *Bonanza*. Don't remember those shows? How about they went out with thinking a gas-guzzling car made sense?
- Thinking knowing people's family issues and understanding their personal lives and problems isn't worth your time. How many times do you have to read our research to get this one?
- Believing that the company, foundation, or organization is what is number one in people's minds and hearts. It definitely is not. Again, we can't say this enough—people have definitely changed in this area. 7/7/05 reinforced it.
- Being afraid to confront reality, thinking people will panic, quit, or otherwise act out. They likely know more than you think they do, and what they want is reality and a plan of action. They want to know what you and they together can DO about what is going on, they want a plan to get moving on and moving ahead. And if there is no way out, help them with Plan B for their lives and move on. They will.
- Forgetting that every individual counts and always has and always will, even if they don't stay with your organization, or move up the ladder, or have the same career ambitions you do.
- Thinking that the merger won't change anything. Talk about lack of emotional intelligence—this shows you are NOT one of the folks in our survey who are in touch with the realities of corporate life.
- Thinking the new outsourcing initiative won't affect you—after all, you are the management!

In summary, people have changed. You have to know them, work at connecting with them, and make the experience of working with you and for you something positive for them. Don't want to trust them? You are making a mistake. Think they can't handle reality? They can and they will. What they don't want to handle is the inability of management and the leadership team to present viable ways of dealing with the realities of this highly competitive world.

Outsourcing growing? OK, what does that mean for us? Are there other value added things we can do, or do we have to move on? How can you help others to get involved in new ways to grow the company, save resources, and so on—think ahead not behind, and engage people with the realities. They already know the game is changing. Show them you understand too and move forward together. This is the number one most important strategy for managers and leaders at every level.

The Organization

What organization can feel genuinely secure today? Not even churches can, or charities or industry leaders. Wal-Mart is worried about their share of business, and they literally invented the modern supply chain as we know it and excelled in it everywhere. But they have issues, it comes with the territory and with being an organization made up of people who are flawed as we all are. Mistakes are made, opportunities are lost, challenges are missed, and carelessness is overlooked—not just at Wal-Mart but also in EVERY single organization out there.

What's an organization to do? This research effort implies that time is ripe for adding reflection to the list of to-dos nearly on a daily or weekly basis. Reflection on what has happened and what you are learning from what you are doing. We are running so fast we have both individually and collectively lost our ability to pause and think. The concept of the learning organization introduced by Peter Senge in the 1990s never really took off, though his forward thinking and original book *The Fifth Discipline* (1990) became a business bestseller, and his expertise and concepts are still popular in the development literature. Perhaps one of the reasons it did not take off (other than it seemed too academic rather than practical) was that workers were not ready to actively participate in the processes needed to make the strategy a reality. They did not have enough understanding of the deep need for change and new and different approaches to deal with globalization—but now, things are different and people are different too.

Senge, and later his many colleagues and other educational and adult education leaders such as Victoria Marsick from Columbia University, recommended that organizations become learning centers. These scholars suggested, based on research into what successful organizations were doing, that the most successful learned and moved forward based on that combination of individual and organizational learning. Work is seen as an opportunity to learn, with the purpose of growing/changing/evolving the organization and the individuals. Better processes, more efficient relationships, better products, and willingness to experiment are all the result of shared responsibility for learning and doing in an integrated way that allows for involvement, experimentation, and reflection.

As a company learns, it develops, and as it develops it meet new needs, seeks new markets, understands new opportunities, and so it goes. We know this is radical—because we know that most organizations do not have the emotional, intellectual, and financial commitment to make it work—but they could if they understood that given where people are now, based on our research, it would have a great chance of success. If adapted to any organization, the integration of personal and organizational learning, coupled with the solving of real and genuine problems and challenges, will result in the very best solutions and new opportunities for the most people and the organization.

We are recommending a broader adoption (there are, of course, organizations, like BP for example, who have embraced this strategy using it to tremendous advantage) of this nearly 15-year old strategy since our research has made clear that people are now READY for the learning organization. First, they are more open to change and willing to risk growing. Second, they are more emotionally intelligent than previously thought and perhaps were. And finally, but no less importantly, the development of Globalization 3.0 created the conditions and the technology to make the learning organization both more doable and more practical than ever before. Here is what is IN and OUT for organizations as they embark on organizational change initiatives and transformation programs, and based on our insights into the Big Picture, the myth of change resistance, and the in-depth analysis of organizational change readiness.

What's IN:

- Transparency. Trying to keep things close to the vest? Not really possible or sensible given technology. The fact that people are more aware of realities plus the increased access to information makes this old stand by of business wisdom totally doable now. Don't delay any longer.
- Reality-based decision making. You can't spin people who can access the facts as quickly as you can.
- Involvement of all stakeholders with full awareness that people will not flip out, flake out, or otherwise act out if the truth is presented appropriately and with respect and consideration for the views and values of the individual participants.
- Better trained, educated leaders supported by a senior leadership team that is working as a team, collaborating and modeling the way. Not spending money on leadership development as an expense control device is outdated in today's complex world. You cannot afford to have unaware and ineffective leaders in complex organizations that are pushing empowerment down the line.
- Process improvements that will allow focus on core competencies.
- More out/in or other sourcing as needed and necessary.
- More horizontal communication. People want to communicate and are good at it if you set the processes in place to encourage it easily. More IM (instant messaging) might be a good thing.
- More allowances and acceptance and celebration of differences. Using diversity for advantages in every aspect of the business. But again, given our data, stress diversity of mind and ideas not the superficial indicators of

age, race, and other externals we didn't see making much of a difference in people at work.

- Focus on what is important, concrete, and specific, and less on hoopla, big time meetings, and rallies to cover the obvious.
- More time spent in teams actually accomplishing things.
- More collaboration, and, finally, the death forever of the internal customer. There is only one customer—of the enterprise—everyone else should be collaborating. There are lots of stakeholders but only one customer. If everyone doesn't have that same customer in mind, you have problems.
- Straight talk. Again, with people as sophisticated as they are, they are not going to handle silly talk and spin. Get real—people are.
- Empowered individuals who know what is important, what is expected, what the rules and standards are, and are given the tools to do it. Again, see the obvious of how people have evolved and now are in touch with things that even a few years ago they would not be.
- The most flexibility and free time possible given the vision and mission.
- The least nonsense possible given people working in-group.
- Consultants, vendors, customers, maybe even the competition aligning and collaborating for value. Again, some people may resist but the more sophisticated vendors and suppliers as well as customers and competition will jump at the chance to collaborate in ways that grow the pie for everyone.

What's OUT:

- The warfare metaphors. The constant competition metaphors. It is about value, customers, innovation, successful connections, meeting needs, and all those things that add not subtract from life and business.
- The sense of us against them. Where there is a focus on losers, the organization loses. This is the biggest reason to avoid any and all reality type events and approaches which are just ways of making some people losers. Real companies and real organizations focus their energies on creating success not weeding out losers. Why bother? Most people want to work hard and get the organization on a positive track—those that aren't should leave but let them self select out by making the culture strong.
- Bad, stupid, and arrogant leadership styles.
- Secrecy. Strategic plans nobody can figure out and that no one buys into.
- Change that is not important and avoiding the realities of the competition or the organization's flaws that everyone knows about. Again, people based on our research are reading what's out there and public knowledge—what are you hiding?
- Believing your business is somehow immune from the rules of decency, competition, the universe, or globalization.

- Thinking the stock price is more important than customers, products, and the people who work for the organization. Jail is not a good thing.
- A culture of no feedback, poor feedback, or kicking down the ladder.

In summary, the organization has to embrace the new as much as individuals and leaders do. Since your workforce is by majority more sophisticated your strategies and approaches have to match that. With a learning approach there is a framework for doing this that is simple, straightforward, and includes all the stakeholders as well as the customers. Connection and collaboration are the name of the game.

Organizational life has never been easy. Individual growth and development has always been challenging even with commitment, help from professionals, and a desire to turn one's situation around. But individuals keep moving ahead and so do organizations. Leaders and managers have always been up against it fighting to keep their own jobs, and trying to manage people or lead them without fully knowing how best to do that.

Life and work have always been difficult. But our research shows hope—strong hope. It implies that despite the horrors of 9/11 or 7/7, the continuing threats and promises of globalization, the difficult challenges of working in organizations that are always demanding more with less, people are definitely rising to the occasion. They embrace change; they know they need to work hard at their own lives and to work at the relationships in their organizations. They have not just the right attitudes but the right behaviors if they are led and given the opportunity to work in organizations that tap into their maturity and interdependence. That suggests to us that the challenges ahead can be met, and that the next generation can clearly move beyond the progress made to date. Maybe all the work we in the development fields have done all these years has meant more than we know—all of us in the workplace now deserve some solace in knowing we have made inroads into developing the world's most important asset—its working people.

PAT GILL WEBBER

POST SCRIPT

As this book goes to press, the tragedy of Hurricane Katrina (which hit the Gulf Coast in early September 2005) and its aftermath is weeks old.

Few who heard about the hurricane were not touched by the scope of the disaster as well as the failure of state, local, and federal government to deal with its devastation on a timely basis. The results of poor listening to repeated warnings, poor sharing of relevant information, and in general poor leadership speak to the tremendous need for more powerful and effective individual excellence and leadership of all institutions as we continue in the 21st century.

If our research is accurate, and our thinking confirmed, the many people affected by the storm will rise to the occasion. They will know that that they need to change, they need to move forward, and they need to strive and thrive post this tragedy. Listening to the many voices on the media, one is struck by just how accurate this analysis is for the majority of evacuees and their families. While some small number of survivors, due to multiple limitations of wealth, education, and/or opportunity will be "lost" or unable to move forward, the vast majority of citizens of all races, backgrounds, and abilities will demonstrate an essentially pro-change and forward-thinking approach to the enormous challenges they face. We have no doubt their emotional intelligence will support their efforts to create new lives that will enrich and fulfill them, whether they chose to relocate permanently or eventually return home to New Orleans and other places on the Gulf Coast once they are rebuilt.

Our concerns are for leaders everywhere. To those doing their jobs with skill and grace, we congratulate you. For those who failed because they lacked the credentials, training, or competence to lead in crisis, we say shame on those who prevented these leaders from getting the training and support they needed to succeed.

Hurricane Katrina is another part of living in a post 9/11 world. Tragedies like this reinforce the need to focus on one's family which we found was a result of living and working in a post 9/11 world. But tragedies also tap into the enormous generosity and ability of people to collaborate and move collectively forward for the common good. The "culture wars" are exaggerated and were, in fact, pushed aside by a common set of values that insisted that we must and can serve all of our citizens in times of need. We hope our small effort in this book to further support positive change, leadership development, learning in organizations, and personal discipline and skill helps to contribute to a more accountable government and a renewed progressive approach to work in the 21st century.

Dr. Pat Gill Webber
Biographical Summary

Dr. Pat Gill Webber is an expert on personal and organizational change. She specializes in working with individuals to lead change initiatives, or companies attempting to implement challenging change strategies from quality improvements to new organizational strategies. She is also considered an expert on leadership and leadership development. She recently co-authored an article "Leadership: Beyond the Baseline" with Catherine Rezak, Founder and CEO of Paradigm Learning, a company specializing in programs dealing with change and innovation in the workplace.

Dr. Gill Webber has over 25 years of experience as a consultant, educator, and executive coach. She has worked with dozens of well known organizations like Wal-Mart, Citigroup, AT&T, and the Federal Reserve Bank of St. Louis, and most recently with Callaway Golf Company, Johnson & Johnson, The Christopher Reeve Foundation, The Quality Assurance Institute, and the Toy Industry Association. She is known as a straightforward, direct, and effective consultant and coach who has both academic and practical credentials.

Dr. Gill Webber is the founder and President of AlexisGill, Inc., a 20 year old virtual consulting firm specializing in working with organizations on issues of change. Dr. Gill Webber is also a partner and co-founder of E-Coach Associates, Inc., which is a specialty coaching firm with a focus on both face-to-face and electronic coaching. To learn more about AlexisGill, Inc., go to www.alexisgill.com. To learn more about E-Coach Associates, Inc., go to www.e-coachonline.com.

Dr. Gill Webber has a master's degree from New York University in counseling psychology and a master's degree in business administration from Fordham University. She received her doctorate in leadership and organizational change from Columbia University in 1998.

Dr. Gill Webber can be reached at 1-800-869-4455, through her website www.drpatgill.com, or at her email, patgillwebber@drpatgill.com.

PART V

Resources

SYNOPSIS

There are four parts to this resource section. The first section is a short appendix that describes details of the statistical analysis completed in phase two of the research for this book. For any additional questions regarding the analysis, please send an email inquiry to patgillwebber@drpatgill.com.

Following the appendix is the reference bibliography which includes all the books or articles mentioned in the text of the book. This is followed by a resource bibliography that contains additional books that might be helpful in considering other aspects of the issue of workers in the early part of the 21st century. Finally, post both bibliographies is the index for easy reference to topics in the text.

Statistics Appendix

The purpose of this part of the book is to offer some details of the statistical analysis involving the second phase of the research. The information provided below is focused around the two major variables presented earlier of gender and age categories on the sub-scores from the Change Reaction (CR) and Emotional Competence Inventory (ECI).

In an effort to examine whether there were statistical differences in the mean responses to each sub-score of the CR and each cluster score of the ECI, a MANOVA was performed on the three sub-scores of the CR and four cluster scores of the ECI as a function of gender and age-category. Please note that because the cluster scores showed higher internal consistency than the competencies, the four cluster scores from the ECI were used in these analyses. Before the MANOVA was undertaken, the data was examined to ensure that the assumptions of the MANOVA were met.

In examining the assumptions, 127 out of the 468 cases (27%) with complete data (i.e., demographic and sub-scores on both scales) were found to be multivariate outliers. These were found by calculating the Mahalanobis distances for the seven sub-scores and clusters, and then finding those distances that were significant using a chi-square distribution at an alpha level of 0.001. Because we wanted to undertake a MANOVA, we examined the existence of these multivariate outliers for each gender and age category. In terms of gender, 68% of the outliers were female. In terms of age category, 42% were 51+, 40% were 36-50, and 18% were 18-35. Because 27% of the cases represented a large number to remove from the analyses and because the outliers tended to be in certain groups (i.e., females above 35 years of age), univariate examinations of each scale were undertaken and transformations were applied. Each of the seven sub-scales was found to be significantly skewed, except for the neutral sub-scale in the CR. After applying transformations to five of the seven variables, six cases were found to be multivariate outliers. These six cases were removed from the subsequent MANOVA analysis. The assumption of homogeneity of variances and covariances was met using Box' test.

The MANOVA using Wilks' lambda showed significant main effects of age category ($F_{(14,1238)}=2.590$, $p<.05$) and gender ($F_{(7,619)}=5.584$, $p<.05$) with the interaction as not being significant ($F_{(14,1238)}=.865$, $p>.05$). Thus, overall, there were statistically significant differences in respondents' sub-scores of the CR and cluster scores of the ECI. The large sample size is probably contributing to this, because the effect sizes using eta-squared were quite small (0.028 and 0.059 for age category and gender, respectively).

Follow-up analyses using ANOVA showed that only the resistant score-score in the CR showed a statistically significant difference across age categories $(F(2,625)=7.257, p <.05)$. Interestingly, the 18-35 category had a large mean of 7.5 than the 36-50 of 6.6 than the 51+ of 6.2 on the resistant sub-score of the CR. Thus, the older age category did not endorse being resistant as the younger ones. Although this is statistically significant, the small effect size suggests these mean differences are not that large.

Additionally, the supportive $(F(1,625)=9.265, p <.05)$ and neutral $(F(1,625)=14.416, p <.05)$ sub-scores in the CR were statistically significant. Males were slightly more supportive and less neutral. The self-management $(F(1,625)=6.597, p<.05)$ and relationship management $(F(1,625)=12.837. p<.05)$ clusters of the ECI showed statistical significance across gender as well. Males showed slightly higher scores. Unfortunately, in all of these statistically significant effects, the large sample size probably contributed to the statistical significance, because the effect sizes using eta-square were all less than 0.023.

A separate analysis was undertaken to examine if there were differences on the CR and ECI by company. A MANOVA found that there were no statistically significant differences across companies on the CR and ECI.

REFERENCE BIBLIOGRAPHY

Axelrod, Richard. (2000). *Terms of Engagement: Changing the Way We Change Organizations.* San Francisco, CA: Berrett-Koehler Publishers, Inc.

Bakke, Dennis W. (2005). *Joy at Work: A Revolutionary Approach to Fun on the Job.* Seattle, WA: PVG.

Barker, Joel A. (1993). *Paradigms: Business of Discovering the Future.* New York, NY: HarperCollins Publisher, Inc.

Cohen, Robert. "The World: The War on Terror; An Obsession the World Doesn't Share." *The New York Times.* 5 December, 2004.

Collins, Jim. (2001). *Good to Great: Why Some Companies Make the Leap...and Others Don't.* New York, NY: Harper-Collins Publisher, Inc.

Covey, Stephen R. (2004). *The 8th Habit: From Effectiveness to Greatness.* New York, NY: Free Press, Davison of Simon & Schuster, Inc.

Covey, Stephen R. (1989). *Seven Habits of Highly Effective People: Powerful Lessons in Personal Change.* New York, NY: Free Press, Division of Simon & Schuster, Inc.

Cranton, Patricia. (1994). *Understanding and Promoting Transformative Learning: A Guide for Educators of Adults.* San Francisco, CA: Jossey-Bass, Inc.

Effron, Marc; Gandossy, Robert; Goldsmith, Marshall. (2003). *Human Resources in the 21st Century.* Hoboken, NJ: John Wiley & Sons, Inc.

Esen, Efren. (2004). *SHRM/CNNfun Job Satisfaction Series: Job Satisfaction Survey Report 2004.* Alexandria, VA: Human Resource Management (SHRM).

Frank, Thomas. (2004). *What's the Matter with Kansas?: How Conservatives Won the Heart of America.* New York, NY: Metropolitan Books.

Friedman, Thomas L. (2003). *Longitudes and Attitudes: The World in the Age of Terrorism.* New York, NY: Alfred A. Knopf, Inc.

Friedman, Thomas L. (2005). *The World Is Flat: A Brief History of the Twenty-first Century.* New York, NY: Farrar, Straus and Giroux

Gardner, Howard. (2004). *Changing Minds: The Art and Science of Changing Our Own and Other People's Minds.* Boston, MA: Harvard Business School Press.

Goleman, Daniel. (1998). *Working with Emotional Intelligence.* New York, NY: Bantam Books.

Goleman, Daniel; McKee, Annie; Boyatzis, Richard E. (2002). *Primal Leadership: Realizing the Power of Emotional Intelligence.* Boston, MA: Harvard Business School Press.

Gordon, Edward E. "The 2010 Crossroads." Training, Jan. 2005. http://www.dolce.com/meetings/article-016-2010-crossroads.php

Hira, Ron and Anil. *Outsourcing America: What's Behind Our National Crisis and How We Can Reclaim American Jobs.* (2005). Amacon.

Joyce, William; Nohria, Nitin. (2003). *What Really Works: The 4+2 Formula for Sustained Business Success.* New York, NY: Harper-Collins Publisher, Inc.

Judis, John B.; Teixeria, Ruy. (2004). *The Emerging Democratic Majority.* New York, NY: Simon & Schuster.

Keagan, Robert. (1995). *In Over Our Heads: The Mental Demands of Modern Life.* Cambridge, MA: Harvard University Press.

Kuhn, Thomas S. (1996). *The Structure of Scientific Revolutions.* Chicago, IL: University of Chicago Press.

Lancaster, Lynne C.; Stillman, David. (2002). *When Generations Collide: Who They Are. Why They Clash. How to Solve the Generational Puzzle at Work.* New York, NY: HarperCollins Publishers, Inc.

Mankin, Don; Cohen, Susan G. (2004). *Business Without Boundaries: An Action Framework for Collaborating Across Time, Distance, Organization, and Culture.* San Francisco, CA: Jossey-Bass.

Maslow, Abraham. (1987 3rd Edition). *Motivation and Personality.* New York, NY: HarperCollins Publisher, Inc.

Mezirow, Jack. (1990). *Fostering Critical Reflection in Adulthood: A Guide to Transformative and Emancipatory Learning.* San Francisco, CA: Jossey-Bass, Inc. Publishers.

Raines, Claire. (2003). *Connecting Generations: The Sourcebook for a New Workplace.* Berkley, CA: Crisp Publications, Inc.

Salopek, Jennifer J. "Engaging Mind, Body, and Spirit at Work." Training and Development. Nov. 2004. http://store.astd.org/product.asp?prodid=2909&deptid=

Schlender, Brent. "Peter Drucker Sets Us Straight (On jobs, debt, globalization, and recession)." *Fortune Magazine. 12 Oct. 2003. http://www.freerepublic.com/focus/f-news/1051078/posts*

Senge, Peter. (1990). *The Fifth Discipline.* New York, NY: Doubleday.

Tabb, William K. (2004). "Globalization." *Microsoft Encarta Online Encyclopedia.* MSN. 1 Aug. 2005. *http://encarta.msn.com/encyclopedia_1741588397/Globalization.html*

Watkins, Karen E. (1991). *Facilitating Learning in the Workplace.* New York, NY: Hyperion Books.

Zemke, Ron; Raines, Claire; Filipczak, Bob. (1999). *Generations at Work: Managing the Clash of Veterans, Boomers, Xers, and Nexters in Your Workplace.* New York, NY: American Management Association.

.

RESOURCE BIBLIOGRAPHY

ORGANIZATIONAL CHANGE AND TRANSFORMATION

Ackerman Anderson, Linda; Anderson, Dean. (2001). *The Change Leader's Roadmap: How to Navigate Your Organization's Transformation.* New York, NY: John Wiley & Sons, Inc.

Alkhafaji, Abbass F. (2000). *Corporate Transformation and Restructuring: A Strategic Approach.* Westport, CT: Greenwood Publishing Group, Inc.

Allen-Meyer, Glenn (2000). *Nameless Organizational Change. No Hype, Low Resistance Corporate Transformation.* Saratoga Springs, NY: Talwood-Craig Publishing Company.

Barabba, Vincent P. (2004). *Surviving Transformation: Lessons from GM's Surprising Turnaround.* New York, NY: Oxford University Press.

Berger, Lance A.; Sikora, Martin J. (1994). *The Change Management Handbook: A Road Map to Corporate Transformation.* New York, NY: McGraw-Hill Professional Book Group.

Bhambri, A.; Alessandro Sinatra. (1997). *Corporate Transformation.* Norwell, MA: Kluwer Academic Publisher.

Bossidy, Larry; Charan, Ram; Burck, Charles. (2002). *Execution: The Discipline of Getting Things Done.* New York, NY: The Crown Publishing Group.

Bridges, William. (1991). *Managing Transitions: Making the Most of Change.* Cambridge, MA: Perseus Publishing.

Burke, W. Warner. (2002). *Organization Change: Theory and Practice.* Thousand Oaks, CA: SAGE Publications.

Chan Allen, Rebecca; Bechard, Richard. (2001). *Guiding Change Journeys: A Synergistic Approach to Organization Transformation.* New York, NY: John Wiley & Sons, Inc.

Duck, Jeanie Daniel. (2001). *The Change Monster: The Human Forces that Fuel or Foil*

Corporate Transformation and Change. New York, NY: Crown Publishing Group.

Espejo, Raul. (1996). *Organizational Transformation and Learning: A Cybernetic Approach to Management.* New York, NY: John Wiley & Sons, Inc.

Fletcher, Beverly. (1990). *Organizational Transformation Theorists and Practitioners.* Westport, CT: Greenwood Publishing Group, Inc.

French, Wendell; Bell, Cecil H.; Zawacki, Robert A. (2004). *Organizational Development and Transformation: Managing Effective Change.* Sixth edition. New York, NY: McGraw
Hill/Irwin.

Fry, Ronald; Barrett, Frank; Seiling, Jane G.; Whitney, Diana. (2001). *Appreciative Inquiry and Organizational Transformation: Reports from the Field.* Westport, CT: Greenwood Publishing Group, Inc.

Green, Thad B.; Butkus, Raymond T. (1999). *Motivation, Beliefs, and Organizational Transformation.* Westport, CT: Greenwood Publishing Group, Inc.

Hambrick, Donald C.; Nadler, David A.; Tushman, Michael. (1997). *Navigating Change: How CEOs, Top Teams, and Boards Steer Transformation.* Boston, MA: Harvard Business School Publishing.

Hey, Kenneth. (2001). *The Caterpillar Doesn't Know: How Personal Change is Creating Organizational Change.* Riverside, CA: Renaissance Books.

Kegan, Robert; Laskow Lahey, Lisa. (2000). *How the Way We Talk Can Change the Way We Work: Seven Languages for Transformation.* New York, NY: John Wiley & Sons, Inc.

Kleiner, Art; Roth, George. (2000). *Oil Change: Perspectives on Corporate Transformation.* New York, NY: Oxford University Press.

Kotter, John P. (1996). *Leading Change.* Watertown, MA: Harvard Business School Press.

Kotter, John P.; Cohen, Dan S. (2002). *The Heart of Change: Real-Life Stories of How People Change Their Organizations.* Watertown, MA: Harvard Business School Press.

Linder, Jane C. (2004). *Outsourcing for Radical Change: A Bold Approach to Enterprise*

Transformation. New York, NY: AMACOM.

Lynton, Rolf P.; Pareek, Udai. (2000). *Training for Organizational Transformation: For Policy-Makers and Change Managers.* Thousand Oaks, CA: Sage Publications, Inc.

Nadler, David A.; Shaw, Robert B.; Walton, A. Elise. (1995). *Discontinuous Change: Leading Organizational Transformation.* San Francisco, CA: Jossey-Bass Publishers.

Persico, John, Jr. (1992). *The TQM Transformation. A Model for Organizational Change.* New York, NY: Productivity Press, Inc.

Smith Blancett, Suzanne; Flarey, Dominick. (1995). *Reengineering Nursing and Health Care: The Handbook for Organizational Transformation.* New York, NY: Aspen Publishers Inc.

Taffinder, Paul. (1998). *Big Change: A Route-Map for Corporate Transformation.* Hoboken, NJ: John Wiley & Sons, Inc.

Vollmann, Thomas E. (1996). *The Transformation Imperative: Achieving Market Dominance through Radical Change.* Boston, MA: Harvard Business School Press.

Whitsett, David A.; Burling, Irving R. (1996). *Achieving Successful Organizational Transformation.* Westport, CT: Greenwood Publishing Group, Inc.

Wycoff, Joyce; Richardson, Tim. (1995). *Transformation Thinking: Tools and Techniques that Open the Door to Powerful New Thinking for Every Member of Your Organization.* New York, NY: Berkley Publishing Group.

Yates, Joanne; Van Maanen, John. (2000). *Information Technology and Organizational Transformation: History, Rhetoric, and Practice.* Thousand Oaks, CA: Sage Publications, Inc.

PERSONAL CHANGE AND TRANSFORMATION

Adrienne, Carol. (2003). *When Life Changes or You Wish it Would: A Guide to Finding Your Next Step Despite Fear, Obstacles, or Confusion.* New York, NY: Perennial Currents.

Adizes, Ichak: Griffin, Patrick H. (1992). *Mastering Change: The Power of Mutual Trust and Respect in Personal Life, Business, and Society.* Santa Barbara, CA: Adizes Institute Publications.

Barrick, Marilyn C. (2000). *Sacred Psychology of Change: Life as a Voyage of Transformation.* Gardiner, Montana: Summit University Press.

Bragg, Terry (1997). *31 Days to High Self-Esteem: How to Change Your Life so You Have Joy, Bliss, and Abundance.* Salt Lake City, UT: Peacemakers Training.

Campbell, Joseph. (2004). *Pathways to Bliss: Mythology and Personal Transformation.* Novato, CA: New World Library.

Christie, Nancy. (2004). *The Gifts of Change.* Hillsboro, OR: Beyond Words Publishing.

Cury, Augusto. (2005). *You are Irreplaceable: Change the Way You Look at Your Life.* Riverside, NJ: Andrews McMeel Publishing.

Dodd, David. (1996). *Playing it Straight: Personal Conversations on Recovery, Transformation, and Success.* Deerfield Beach, Florida: Health Communications, Inc.

Dyer, Wayne W. (2001). *You'll See It When You Believe It: The Way to Personal Transformation.* New York, NY: Perennial Currents.

Earley, Jay. (1990). *Inner Journeys: A Guide to Personal and Social Transformation Based on the Work of Jean Houston.* York Beach, ME: Red Wheel.

Ferguson, Marilyn. (1980). *The Aquarian Conspiracy: Personal & Social Transformation of Our Time.* New York, NY: Putnam Publishing Group.

Fishel, Ruth. (2001). *Change Almost Anything in 21 Days.* Martstonsmills, MA: Spirithaven.

Gawain, Shakti. (2000). *The Path of Transformation: How Healing Ourselves Can Change the World.* Novato, CA: New World Library.

Goodier, Steve. (2002). *Lessons of the Turtle.* Salt Lake City, UT: Life Support System Publishing.

Manning, George (1998). *Stress: Living and Working in a Changing World.* Duluth, MN: Whole Person Associates, Inc.

Maxwell, John C. (2003). *Thinking for a Change: 11 Ways Highly Successful People Approach Life and Work.* New York, NY: Warner Books, Inc.

McKenzie, Vashti M. (2003). *Journey to the Well: 12 Lessons on Personal Transformation.* New York, NY: Penguin Books.

McWaters, Barry; Gordon, Janet. (1981). *Conscious Evolution: Personal & Planetary Transformation.* Snowflake, Arizona: New Age Press, Inc.

Myss, Caroline; Gawain, Shakti. (2000). *Second Edition. The Path of Transformation: How Healing Ourselves Can Change the World.* Novato, CA: New World Library.

Porter, L. Joe; Porter, Joe, M.D. (2001). *Simple Changes: The Boomer's Guide to a Healthier, Happier Life.* Omaha, NE: Addicus Books.

Prober, Paula. (2001). *Ten Tips for Women Who Want to Change the World Without Losing their Friends, Shirts, or Minds.* Eugene, OR: T.C.C. Press.

Reiss, Gary. (2000). *Changing Ourselves, Changing the World.* Tempe, AZ: New Falcon Publications.

Rubino, Dr. Joe. (2004). *The Legend of the Light-Bearers: A Fable About Personal Reinvention and Global Transformation.* Boxword, MA: Vision Works Publishing.

Scott, Ph.D., Cynthia D.; Jaffe, Ph.D., Dennis T. (2004). *Managing Personal Change: Moving Through Personal Transition (Crisp Fifty-Minute Series).* Boston, MA: Crisp Publications.

Spencer, Sabina A.; Adams, John D. (1990). *Life Changes: Growing Through Personal Transitions.* Atascadero, CA: Impact Publishers, Inc.

Tirabassi, Becky. (2003). *Keep the Change: Breaking Through to Permanent Transformation.* Brentwood, TN: Integrity Publishers.

Vanzant, Iyanla. (2001). *Iyanla Live Volume 7 Transformation.* New York, NY: Simon & Schuster Audio.

Wicks, Robert J. (2000). *Simple Changes: Quietly Overcoming Barriers to Personal and Professional Growth.* Allen, TX: Thomas More Association.

Wolford, Dudley. (1999). *Your Time for Change: How to be the Best You Can Become.* Sisters, OR: Brentwood Productions.

Zoglio, Suzanne. (2000). *Create a Life that Tickles Your Soul: Finding Peace, Passion, & Purpose.* Doylestown, PA: Tower Hill Press.

POST 9/11

Agosin, Marjorie; Craige, Betty Jean. (2002). *To Mend the World: Women Reflect on 9/11*. Buffalo, NY: White Pine Press.

Bethel, Tony (2003). *Before Forty After 9/11: Poems from the Heart Land*. Bloomington, IN: Authorhouse.

Campbell, Benjamin P. *On the Sabbath After: Messages of Hope Delivered on the Sabbath After September 11, 2001: A Tribute to the Victims and Their Families*. Richmond, VA: Brandylane Publishers, Inc.

Chepak, Mary Ellen. (2002). *Coping After 9/11 and Beyond: An Everyday Handbook*. New York, NY: Mary Ellen Chepak CSW.

Cortada, James W.; Wakin, Edward. (2002). *Betting on America: Why the U.S. Can Be Stronger After September 11*. London: New York: Financial Times/Prentice Hall.

Friedman, Thomas L. (2002). *Longitudes and Attitudes: Exploring the World After September 11*. New York, NY: Farrar, Straus and Giroux.

Greenberg, Judith. (2003). *Trauma at Home: After 9/11*. Lincoln, NE: University of Nebraska Bison Books.

Hazen, Don (2002). *After 9/11: Solutions for a Saner World*. San Francisco, CA: Last Gasp.

Margolis, Joseph. (2004). *Moral Philosophy After 9/11*. University Park, PA: Pennsylvania State University Press.

Precin, Pat. (2004). *Surviving 9/11: Impact and Experiences of Occupational Therapy Practioners*. Binghamton, NY: The Haworth Press, Inc.

Dixon, Wheeler Winston. (2004). *Film and Television After 9/11*. Carbondale, IL: Southern Illinois University Press.

STARTING OVER

Charland, William A. (1993). *Career Shifting: Starting Over in a Changing Economy.* Avon, MA: Adams Media Corporation.

Danna, Jo. (1990). *Starting Over: You in the New Workplace.* Briarwood, NY: Palomino Press.

Gray, John. (1999). *Mars and Venus Starting Over: A Practical Guide for Finding Love Again After a Painful Breakup, Divorce, or the Loss of a Loved One.* New York, NY: HarperCollins Publishers, Inc.

Jasper, James M. (2000). *Restless Nation: Starting Over in America.* Chicago, IL: University of Chicago Press.

Kennedy Dugan, Meg; Hock, Roger R. (2000). *It's My Life Now: Starting Over After an Abusive Relationship or Domestic Violence.* Florence, KY: Taylor & Francis Group/ Routledge.

Kerkstra Harty, Karen. (1991). *50 and Starting Over: Career Strategies for Success.* Franklin Lakes, NJ: Career Press Incorporated.

Kew, Richard. (1994). *Starting Over, But Not from Scratch: Mental and Spiritual Health Between Jobs.* Nashville, TN: Abingdon Press.

Kramon, James. (2004). *Starting Over.* Naperville, IL: Sphinx Publishing Inc.

Jasper, James M. (2002). *Restless Nation: Starting Over in America.* Chicago, IL: University of Chicago Press.

McDonald, Patrick J.; McDonald, Claudette M. (1997). *Out of the Ashes: A Handbook for Starting Over.* Mahwah, NJ: Paulist Press.

Laz, Medard (1998). *Life After the Divorce: Practical Advice for Starting Over.* Liguori, Mo: Liguori Publications.

Montana, Partrick J. (1999). *Stepping Out, Starting Over.* Second edition. Whitby, Ontario: McGraw-Hill Primis Custom Publisher.

Pollan, Stephen M.; Levine, Mark (1997). *Starting Over: How to Change Careers or Start Your Own Business.* Lebanon, IN: Warner Books, Inc.

Skilling Kellerman, Pat. (2004). *Starting Over.* Philadelphia, PA: Xlibris Corporation.

Timmons, Tim; Arterburn, Stephen. (1985). *Hooked on Life: From Stuck to Starting Over.* Nashville, TN: Thomas Nelson, Inc.

Whiteman, Thomas. (1997). *Fresh Start: 8 Principles for Starting Over When Your Relationships Don't Work.* Carol Stream, IL: Tyndale House Publishers.

INDEX